ANDREW ZIMMERN'S FIELD GUIDE TO EXCEPTIONALLY WEIRD, WILD, & WONDERFUL FOODS

ANDREW ZIMMERN'S FIELD GUIDE TO EXCEPTIONALLY WEIRD, WILD, & WONDERFUL FOODS

AN INTREPID EATER'S DIGEST

BY **ANDREW ZIMMERN**

AND **MOLLY MOGREN**

ILLUSTRATIONS BY CHUCK GONZALES

FEIWEL AND FRIENDS • NEW YORK

To Noah, whose love of all things weird, wild,
and wonderful make him the most intrepid eater I know.
—A. Z.

To picky eaters everywhere:
I used to be one of you and now I eat blood sausage for breakfast.
Don't be afraid. It's just food. —M. M.

A FEIWEL AND FRIENDS BOOK
An Imprint of Macmillan

ANDREW ZIMMERN'S FIELD GUIDE TO EXCEPTIONALLY WEIRD, WILD, AND WONDERFUL FOODS.
Copyright © 2012 by Andrew Zimmern. Illustrations copyright © 2012 by Chuck Gonzales. All rights reserved.
Printed in the United States of America by R. R. Donnelley & Sons Company, Crawfordsville, Indiana.
For information, address Feiwel and Friends, 175 Fifth Avenue, New York, N.Y. 10010.

Library of Congress Cataloging-in-Publication Data Is Available

ISBN: 978-1-250-01929-5 (hardcover)
10 9 8 7 6 5 4 3 2 1

ISBN: 978-0-312-60661-9 (paperback)
10 9 8 7 6 5 4 3 2 1

Book design by April Ward

Feiwel and Friends logo designed by Filomena Tuosto

First Edition: 2012

mackids.com

CONTENTS

I WANTED TO READ THIS BOOK WHEN I WAS YOUR AGE.

We just hadn't written it yet.

When I was young, I would sneak into my parents' living room and grab all the oversized books I could find, the more pictures in them, the better. It wasn't that I didn't like reading. I loved reading! It was that I simply wanted to see pictures of things that I didn't know about. I loved old encyclopedias, world record books, fine art and painting books, photography books, travelogues, world histories, sports books, tales of military campaigns, anything about ancient Egypt, and even memoirs of great men. Frankly, the stranger, the better. I liked the stuff no one else was talking about. My imagination devoured those types of stories. From crop circles to the disappearance of the Mayans, from biographies of John Dillinger to the Seven Wonders of the Ancient World, I was swept up in the stories behind the stories. Those tales, the oddities and the unusual, were the ones that allowed me to drift into dreams, to put myself into those worlds, and to spark my imagination.

Most nights, I would sneak those books out of our living room and into my bed. Lying on my stomach under the sheets, flashlight perched on my shoulder, I would inhale my nightly reading list. I miss those days . . . I miss them a lot.

When my son came into my life, I tried to spark

the same fire inside his imagination, and he and I thought it seemed pretty selfish on our part to keep this only to ourselves, so I decided to ignite the same fire in *your* belly, a fire that I think needs to be there. I think you want to know about the world and everything in it. I think you need to know about zombies and dung beetles, about eating hearts and toes, and haggis! And I think dead Scottish poets who devoted their lives to praising this spectacularly tasty treat would interest you in profound ways once you had their indecipherable "Address to a Haggis" translated into a language you can understand! Robert Burns was hysterical—he wrote poems worshipping food cooked inside a sheep's stomach, for crying out loud!

And this book is important for everyone to read because in democratizing the idea of food, in presenting a level playing field where candy, headcheese, scatological treats, brain-sucking zombies, and stinky cheese bugs are all treated as equals, we create a place where everyone from tablecloth dining—obsessed food geeks and ova-lacto-vegans, and even folks like you and I, can all agree is fun to explore and read about. Well, that makes the ultimate egalitarian statement about all foods being equal . . . and we salute our commonality. We respect someone else's ideas about something strange and unusual to us. That's a big idea. When you see a world where we are constantly defining ourselves by our differences, where we see skin color, ethnicity, politics, religion, and spiritual systems as ways to separate the people of our planet into categories, I think we need to shift focus to the things we have in common, such as our love of food. I never liked someone less after sharing a good meal with them.

If we can tell tales, and, through those amazing stories, get excited about food we could never imagine eating, we begin to solve our biggest problem, practicing contempt prior to investigation. That's a fancy way to think about what happens when you tell your mom or dad you don't like a food before you've even tried it. And when we tackle that issue together, we begin to grow a patience and a tolerance, and an understanding of the world around us that will change our world for the better, *your* world for the better . . . and that's pretty darn cool. Start reading.

ANDREW ZIMMERN

ANDREW ZIMMERN'S FIELD GUIDE TO EXCEPTIONALLY WEIRD, WILD, & WONDERFUL FOODS

Alligator Meat

Though we often consider American alligators menacing and fierce, they're truly a creature of wonder. One look at this giant, lizard-like animal conjures an image of something you've only seen in books (or maybe *Jurassic Park*). The dinosaur connection is not just a coincidence—scientists believe gators have roamed the earth for more than 150 million years, managing to well outlive the dinosaurs, who became extinct 65 million years ago. But they are twin sons of different mothers.

What's crazy is that though gators survived the massive meteor or climate change or whatever the heck killed T. rex and company, they were almost snuffed out completely in the 1960s. Loss of habitat, improperly managed wildlife areas, and excessive hunting led to dwindling gator populations, and in 1967, they were put on the endangered species list. Since then, the reptiles have bounced back considerably and were removed from the list in 1987. They still thrive in southeastern America, especially in Florida and Louisiana.

Why Alligator Meat?

Gators may save your life. Okay, so maybe that's a little extreme, but with concerns about cholesterol, fat, and calories, many people are looking for beef alternatives. Chicken and turkey continue to populate tables across the country, but maybe it's time we start eating gator. Sounds weird, but it's true: Gator is one of the healthiest proteins you can feast on. Alligator meat has a fine texture, similar to chicken and pork, but contains less calories, fat, and cholesterol than either of the "other white meats."

If you order gator in a restaurant (or make it at home), what often ends up on your plate comes from the long muscle in the tail. It's also possible to eat gator ribs and wings (which come from those little T. rex–like legs). In some cultures, people often eat the meat raw—but that's not recommended unless the animal is (a) dead and (b) very fresh. Bon appetit!

Now, this is what I call a Cajun cookout! The folks in Bayou Pigeon, LA, roast the gator whole, then eat everything but the paws.

JAWS

Ever since the 1975 cinematic thriller *Jaws*, some of us have been a little afraid to dip our toes in the water. Sharks-schmarks . . . *gators* are the water-lurking species that give me the willies. These carnivores' mouths are stuffed with seventy to eighty teeth, designed for gripping and ripping. They have the most powerful bite in the animal kingdom—3,000 pounds per square inch! Oddly enough, while a gator could literally sever your leg in one chomp, the muscles required to open a gator jaw are wimpy. You could keep their mouths sealed with a thick rubber band (or your hands if you're crazy enough to wrestle one).

HOW TO SURVIVE AN ALLIGATOR ATTACK

Getting stuck in an elevator with seven other people after a chili cook-off is the only thing I can think of that's scarier than an alligator attack. These animals are hungry, powerful, and essentially prehistoric, which makes them some of the baddest boys roaming the earth. Though attacks are uncommon, you're not necessarily doomed if you keep these things in mind:

1. STAY OUT OF HARM'S WAY.
If you're in gatorville (i.e., Florida and Louisiana), don't go swimming at dawn or dusk—a favorite hunting time for these reptilians. Be mindful of alligator nests (typically made with rotting vegetation around the edge of wetlands. These can be up to 3.5 feet high) and keep your distance—if you think your mom can be mean, you don't even want to know what an angry alligator mom is like. Don't ever feed wild gators, no matter how cute they are! This desensitizes them to humans and makes them associate you with lunch, which is what you will be if you keep feeding them.

2. RUN LIKE HECK.
You've probably heard that gators are really fast, both in and out of the water. On land, they can reach a speed of 10 miles per hour. And in the water, well, let's just say that regardless of speed, they can hold their breath a whole lot longer than you can. So if you're in danger of a gator attack, run like heck. You may have heard that it's best to run in a zigzag pattern, but don't. It's important to put as much distance between you and the gator as possible.

3. EYES ON THE PRIZE.
So you didn't listen to any of this advice and now a gator's got your arm. Your best plan of attack is to gouge the reptile's eyes. Jam your thumb into its sockets—this will hopefully blind and disorient the animal, plus it will hurt—a lot. If and when the gator lets go, see step two.

4. ROLL WITH THE PUNCHES.
If you're trapped in a gator's vise grip, expect the animal to start a death roll. This move is not unlike a figure skater's spin—the alligator tucks in its legs and moves its tail to the side. The inertia created by this movement allows the crocodilian to spin, and dismembers its prey in the process. Due to their cone-shaped teeth, alligators can't chew, and instead they rely on this technique to create "bites" small enough to swallow whole. Your last-ditch effort is to attempt to roll in the same direction as the alligator so it doesn't rip off a limb. Best of luck.

GATOR FACT OR FICTION

MYTH: **Temperature determines the sex of a gator.**
FACT! If a gator's eggs are kept at less than 88 degrees the gator will be a female; if it's warmer than 91 degrees it will be a male.

MYTH: **You have to be crazy to wrestle an alligator.**
FACT! No explanation needed.

MYTH: **Alligators make good pets.**
FICTION! Grizzly bears, venomous snakes, and alligators don't make good pets! They aren't cuddly, they won't do any cool tricks, and they're not afraid to take a bite of your finger just to see what you taste like. You want a pet? Get a hermit crab.

MYTH: **Alligators have the most powerful jaws in the animal kingdom.**
FACT! When a gator bites down on something—a fish, turtle, or even wild pig!—the force rivals that of a falling pickup truck.

MYTH: **Momma gators eat their hatchlings.**
FICTION! Though gator cannibalism isn't unheard of, mothers do not eat their young. However, the mother gator will protect her young by carrying them around in her mouth.

MORE BiZarre Truth About Gators

- The biggest alligator ever recorded was 19 feet, 2 inches. That's about the same size as the sleek and saucy 1979 Lincoln Continental. It's double the length of the world's tallest man on record, Robert Wadlow (left). When he passed away at the age of twenty-two, he measured 8 feet, 11 inches and was still growing. And it's the same length as 19.16 foot-long hot dogs.

- Alligators typically live about thirty to fifty years.

- When alligators close their mouths, every fourth tooth fits into a hole in the top jaw.

- The scales on a gator are called scutes, and they create a protective armor.

- Alligators live in a subtropical climate, meaning they live in places with a lot of rain and mild winters.

- To swim, alligators typically tuck their arms and legs in at their sides to create a streamlined shape. They then use their long tails to propel themselves forward.

- When gators go underwater, they have skin flaps that cover their nostrils and throats so they don't inhale water.

- Gators can hold their breath for up to thirty minutes. Sometimes the air in their lungs can cause them to float. Some alligators will swallow rocks to weigh them down in the water. The rocks can also help with digestion.

ALLIGATORS VS. CROCODILES

- While both are from the same family and are called "crocodilians," alligators have smaller snouts and are usually smaller in size.

- While crocodiles can be found around the world, alligators are only native to the United States and Asia.

- Alligators prefer fresh water but sometimes live in brackish water. Crocodiles are typically found in salt water.

- Alligators hibernate in "gator holes"—a den dug with their claws and snout where they can rest during the dry season or winter. Crocodiles don't hibernate.

- Southern Florida is the only place in the wild where both crocodiles and alligators live.

- The teeth of a crocodile and an alligator are arranged differently.

- Both can be found in tropical swamps.

When Life Gives You Gators, Make Gatorade

A gigantic cooler of Gatorade is a football sideline fixture, but what's the story behind this ubiquitous sports drink? (And why in the heck is it called Gatorade?)

In 1965, the University of Florida's assistant football coach wanted to figure out why the heat completely drained his team's energy. He called on the university's physicians to look into the problem. They assembled a research team and discovered two key factors: The fluids and electrolytes the players lost through sweat were not being replaced, and the large amounts of carbohydrates the players' bodies used for energy were not being replenished.

The researchers formulated a new beverage aimed at replacing the carbs and electrolytes lost in sweat. They named their beverage after the team it helped—the Florida Gators. The team saw a difference almost instantly. They started outperforming higher-ranking teams, and the following year they won the Orange Bowl. Other teams (both college and professional) started providing this miracle drink to players. Today, Gatorade can be found on the sidelines of more than seventy Division I colleges. In 1983, Gatorade became the official sports drink of the NFL—a title it holds to this day. It's also the official sports drink of the NBA, AVP, PGA, Major League Baseball, Major League Soccer, and numerous other elite and professional organizations and teams.

THINGS FOUND IN GATORS' BELLIES:

Alligators mostly subsist on a diet of fish, turtles, snakes, small rodents, and birds. However, these animals are omnivorous and will eat pretty much anything they can sink their teeth into. For example:

ROCKS
STICKS
CANS
FISHING LURES
LOTS OF DOG COLLARS

Bird's Nest Soup

Every once in a while I stumble upon a food and think, "What sick mind came up with this idea in the first place?" Bird's nest soup falls into that category. I'd like to meet whoever first decided to soak a bird's nest in water overnight, then pick feathers and feces out of the nest, add it to a bowl of chicken broth, onions, sherry, and egg white, and then start eating. C'mon, that's insane.

The soup's flavor depends largely on the geographic region of the nest. I love nests harvested near the ocean. They offer a sea-salty, briny flavor (the birds eat primarily saltwater fish, the nests are full of their saliva, spewdom, and droppings. It only makes sense that the nests would taste of the sea!). Some chefs like to play up the salty flavor (and sometimes sliminess) of the soup. I'm cool with that. To me, it just tastes like Mom's chicken soup—seasoned with bird spit and lots of slimy chunks.

However, the Chinese (as well as some Taiwanese and Indonesians) have enjoyed this gelatinous, soupy delicacy for hundreds if not over a thousand years. The soup isn't made from any old nest. The soup calls for the nest of a bird called the swiftlet or cave swift. These birds produce special nests found not in trees but in caves throughout southern Asia, the south Pacific islands, and northeastern Australia.

As you can imagine, it's not easy to attach a nest to a cave wall. These industrious birds use a mixture of seaweed, twigs, moss, hair, and feathers to fashion the nest. The truly bizarre secret ingredient: saliva. Male birds gorge themselves on seaweed, which causes them to salivate like a Labradoodle at a picnic. Saliva threads, which contain a bonding protein called mucilage, spew out of the bird's mouth. Once dry, the saliva acts as cement. The crafty avian will continue to build on to the nest until it can support the weight of its bird family. The process usually takes about forty-five days.

Swiftlet Factoids

- The birds live in southern Asia, the south Pacific islands, and northeastern Australia.

- Swiftlets have four toes and short legs, so they cannot perch, but they can cling to vertical surfaces like the side of a cave or their nests.

- A swiftlet's diet is made up of insects and more insects, with insects for dessert.

- Swiftlets mate for life, and both the male and female take care of the babies.

- Swiftlets typically lay one to two eggs.

They say a bird in the hand is worth two in the bush. Since a bowl of bird's nest soup costs about $30, I vote for two nests in the hand!

Want to burn some cash in quick order? Slurp down a bowl of bird's nest soup. The dish, which is most popular in Hong Kong and the United States, typically costs $30 to $100 a pop, which is cheap (no pun intended) compared to some versions of the soup. A kilogram of a white nest can cost up to $2,000, and red nests sometimes fetch $10,000 each. It sounds like a lot, but the most expensive nests are newer and more translucent, meaning they're contaminated with less bird droppings and feathers. The red nests, which are more rare, are known to improve digestive health and boost the immune system. That being said, this is still a very expensive lunch.

Men at Work

Harvesting a swift nest is a dangerous job, but it pays well. Guys in the biz (and it is mostly men) come from a long line of harvesters. Fathers will teach their sons the tricks of the trade.

The nests are found high off the ground, up to 200 feet. Harvesters use rickety bamboo ladders to fetch the nests, then dislodge them with a sharpened bamboo stick. Many harvesters have been severely injured or lost their lives falling off ladders. My advice to you? Become a firefighter, astronaut, Tilt-a-Whirl operator, spelunking guide—pretty much any job is safer than this one!

China may be the world's largest consumer of bird's nest cuisine, but Indonesia is the world's largest producer of swift nests—exporting 500 to 600 tons annually. However, as in the fishing industry, the swift harvesting process needs serious tweaking. While swifts aren't an endangered species, their numbers are dwindling. The main reason: their market price! The nests are basically gold attached to a cave, enticing poachers (and some harvesters) to nab nests before they're finished, or while they have eggs or birds still living in them.

The Indonesian government created regulatory measures to protect the birds. It is illegal to throw away eggs or baby birds in the nests, and popular nesting caves are often protected by armed guards. Some poachers have been killed trying to get a hold of nests. In a few incidents, innocent fishermen have been killed after seeking shelter in the caves during a storm. If you see guards with guns outside a cave in Indonesia, steer clear. These guys aren't fooling around.

Beijing National Stadium

Also known as the "Bird's Nest," Beijing National Stadium was built for the 2008 Summer Olympics. The stadium, designed by Herzog & de Meuron, cost $423 million to build and is considered the world's largest enclosed space. The stadium could hold about 8.5 billion bowls of bird's nest soup. That's a big honkin' bowl!

Echolocation

Swiftlets are very fast and dart around pitch-black caves without crashing and burning. This is due to echolocation, a biological sonar also used by some bats, whales, and dolphins. Here's how it works: An animal will send out a sound and wait for it to bounce back. The sound will come back differently depending on the proximity of the object. Swiftlets use a simple form in which they produce a clicking noise that helps them determine how close objects are in front of them.

Saliva Facts

- Saliva is 98 percent water. The other 2 percent is made up of electrolytes, mucus, antibacterial compounds, and various enzymes.

- Saliva is used in the first part of digestion. It moistens food and starts to break it down with its enzymes. It also helps to create a food bolus to help us swallow. Our mouths, with the help of saliva, roll our chewed food into a ball, so the food goes down the esophagus and not the trachea.

- When you have to vomit, there is a signal sent to your brain and you create extra saliva. This makes the vomit less acidic, protecting your throat, mouth, and teeth from burning and decay.

- The average person makes 700 milliliters of saliva per day. That's the equivalent to more than two cans of soda.

- Your spit production slows down when you sleep.

- The mouth is the most unsanitary part of your body. It houses about 10 billion bacteria.

- Saliva rinses the mouth to reduce the bacteria amount, but at night when its production slows down, there is very little cleaning being done. That's why we often wake up with bad breath. We smell all of the bacteria that have built up overnight. It's mouth B.O.

TO SPIT OR NOT TO SPIT

A "spitball" in baseball was created when an outfielder in 1902 named George Hildebrand told his pitcher Elmer Strickland that if you spit on a baseball it would travel in an unexpected fashion, making it very difficult to hit. The spit creates friction and does not allow the ball to spin.

Now a spitball is illegal in baseball. Anytime a pitcher even touches his mouth, he must wipe his hand before touching the ball.

In China, it is not impolite to spit. The air quality is so poor in the country that many people produce a high amount of mucus and they get rid of it wherever they are.

Watermelon-seed-spitting contests are a popular sport. A Texas man named Lee Wheelis claims he spit one seed 68 feet, 9⅛ inches.

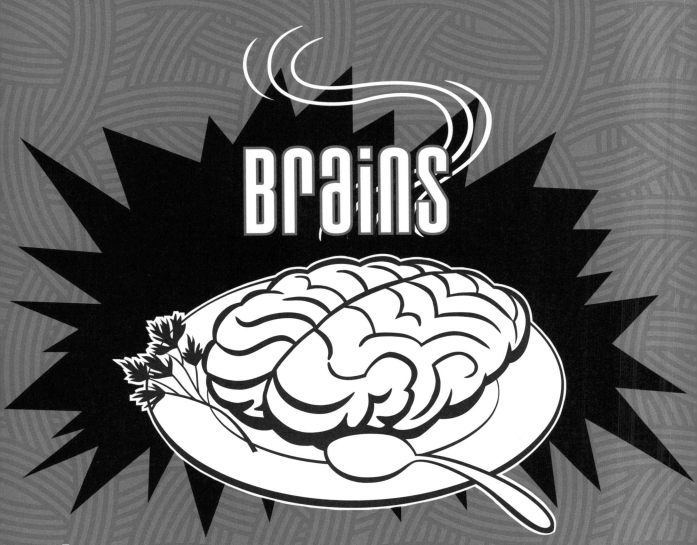

Brains

It may sound straight out of a sci-fi flick, but lamb, pig, and cow brains are popularly eaten around the world. In fact, you can eat pretty much any animal's brain, like squirrel or penguin, provided it's fresh. And I love them all. The first brains I ever ate were calves' brains, sautéed *à la meunière*, or "in the style of the miller"—which means dusted in flour, the pan deglazed with white wine, parsley, and brown butter, and finished with lemon. For me, it's the gold standard of brain preparations, but I also love Thai pig brain soup and West Virginia's roasted squirrel brains cracked out of the skull. Small roasted baby birds' brains from hummingbirds to squab and even small chickens are a special treat. When brains are cooked whole, I can crush the skull between my teeth like a bipedal seal humanoid, reveling in the sweet rush of juicy cranial gray matter as it courses its way down my throat. Yum!

Brains are rich in phosphorous, proteins, and vitamins. Their fat content is one quarter of that in a T-bone steak, but it is extremely high in cholesterol. You might think that brains would be rubbery, but they are actually rather creamy and taste like mushy river rocks mingled with warm pennies. Brains didn't always have a creepy connotation. If you lived in eighteenth-century Europe, it'd be an honor to find brain on your plate. The skull was always sawed in half before roasting so it could be lifted up at the end of the meal. Of course, the brain must be eaten with a spoon—it's impolite to eat the brain with a knife (or, heaven forbid, a spork)!

Feasting on soup made of pig's brain and intestine (with a bit of fish guts for extra flavor!) in Bangkok, Thailand.

PiCK YOUR BRaiN:

Brains are highly perishable, so you want to buy the freshest brains you can find. They should be bright pinkish-white, plump, and firm. Use the same day.

PREPARATION:

- Wash a few small calves' brains, lamb brains, or pig brains in cold water. Remove membranes, spinal cord stem, and any large blood vessels. Soak brains in cold water for about an hour.

- Rinse the brains again. Blanch in simmering salt water for a minute or two to firm, rinse in cool water, and pat dry with paper towel.

- Dredge in seasoned flour.

- Brown well in a hot pan with butter over medium-high heat.

- Add 2 minced shallots and 1 tablespoon each minced tarragon and parsley. Swirl in pan. Add 2 tablespoons drained and rinsed capers.

- Add 1 cup white wine.

- Reduce by two-thirds in volume, spoon brains out of pan, and plate them. Reduce liquid for another moment or so, adding lemon juice to season. Sauce should coat a spoon but not be thick.

- Add sauce and serve.

!ZOMBIE

(\zäm-bē\) noun: a reanimated dead human who scours the planet with an insatiable thirst for human brrrraaaaiiiinssss.

Though I can't find much fault in the diet of zombies (they do eat brains, after all), they are a pesky species that, when left to their own devices, could potentially overtake the world. (At the very least, they could ruin an upcoming birthday party . . . these guys are always stopping by uninvited!)

If you find yourself at the precipice of a zombie attack, it's possible to survive. We talked survival methods with Dr. Robert Smith? (yes, the ? is part of his name) of the University of Ottawa's Department of Mathematics and Faculty of Medicine. Dr. Smith? has dedicated his career to the study of infectious diseases—like malaria, HIV, influenza, and possibly the most terrifying disease of them all—zombies!

HOW TO ▶ Survive a Zombie Outbreak

BY DR. ROBERT SMITH? (yes, the ? is part of his name) of the University of Ottawa

1. GUNS. Don't even bother. These are an illusion of protection, but they're not actually very useful. Ever tried to shoot a moving target? It's really hard! And you don't just have to shoot your zombie in the chest, you have to shoot him in the head, destroying the brain. Unless he's standing on top of you, you're probably not going to hit the head. And if he is standing on top of you, then most likely so are fifteen of his friends, so you have bigger problems. Which brings me to . . .

2. BULLETS. This goes hand in hand with the gun thing. Think about it for a moment.

Civilization has collapsed. Everyone you know is a mindless cannibal. Zombies are surrounding you. Sure, maybe you can shoot a few of them, but what happens when the bullets run out? As they surely will in about twenty-four hours, unless you happen to be holed up in a munitions factory. And even then, do you know how to work and maintain complex bullet-making machinery? I don't. Face it: Sooner or later (okay, sooner), you're going to run out of bullets. And then what do you do?

3. THE MALL. What do we see in every zombie movie? A group of isolated individuals holes up in the mall or a farmhouse, barricading themselves in. This is the worst plan in the history of the universe. What happens next? They bicker and argue with each other, until they make some crucial mistake. Meanwhile, there are five thousand zombies standing outside, just waiting for the stupidest member of the group to accidentally open the door. Remember: You need food, water, and sleep. Zombies only need your brains.

4. WOODEN STAKE to the heart. I think you've mixed up your undead opponents there. That's a mistake that isn't going to end well. Unless you're a zombie, that is.

SO IF ALL THE USUAL TRICKS DON'T WORK, JUST HOW DO WE SURVIVE A ZOMBIE OUTBREAK?

ANSWER: We have something the zombies don't. Celebrities! No, wait, that's not much help, even when there isn't a zombie apocalypse. We have a much better weapon than that: our collective intelligence. We're smarter than they are and—crucially—we're smarter as a group than we are as individuals. We can build walls, electrify fences, and dig moats. We can also research a potential zombie vaccine, dissect deceased zombies to find out how they work and possibly develop a cure. Ever wonder why the zombie apocalypse always involves the end of civilization? It's because that's the biggest threat to the zombies, so they take that down first.

In short, our best defense is civilization and if there's a zombie outbreak the best thing we can do is band together and rebuild it. Because what do zombies fear most? Braaaiiinnnsss.

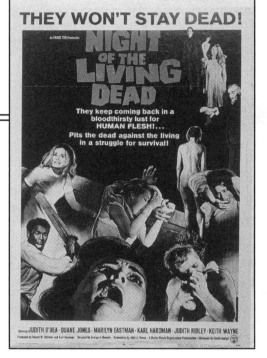

THEY WON'T STAY DEAD!

Night of the Living Dead, created by George A. Romero, was released in 1968.

MYTH: LIVE MONKEY BRAIN!

As seen in *Indiana Jones and the Temple of Doom*, and talked about in a creepy urban myth: Supposedly, live monkeys are strapped into a special table that has holes in the surface. Just the top of the head is on a plate and the skull is sawed. The brain is then consumed with a spoon while the monkey is still living. Not true.

TOP TEN FOODS that are good for your brain!

1. Acai berries
2. Almonds
3. Avocados
4. Bananas
5. Blackberries
6. Blueberries
7. Brewer's yeast
8. Broccoli
9. Brown rice
10. Brussels sprouts

Weird Brain Facts

- The human brain is the fattest organ and can be made up of 60 percent fat.

- There are 100,000 miles of blood vessels in the brain.

- The brain stops growing at age eighteen.

- Children who learn more than one language before age five have different brain structures from adults and have denser gray matter.

- When you're awake, the brain generates between 10 and 23 watts of power, or enough energy to power a lightbulb.

- Harvard has a Brain Bank where they keep more than 7,000 human brains stored for research.

- Humans experience an average of 70,000 thoughts per day. If you're me, 68,000 of them are about food.

- The brain uses 20 percent of the oxygen in your body.

QUESTION:

It's prttey fnuny how we can raed tihs einrte snetnece wtih all tehse ltters all out of palce, and we can cnotniue to keep raednig and sitll mekas snece of waht we are raeding. No mttar how mnay tmies you raed tihs oevr and oevr you can sitll mkae snece of it.

How is taht pssoible?

BRAINIACS

ALBERT EINSTEIN

(March 14, 1879–April 18, 1955)

The Nobel Prize–winning Father of Modern Physics wasn't always synonymous with brilliance. When he was a baby, his own mother thought he was deformed due to his large head, and he showed signs of language impairments at an early age. He didn't speak until the age of three and had difficulty with language and reading throughout school. His teachers even told his parents they believed him to be borderline retarded and that their son would never amount to much.

The German-born scientist never gave up. He continued with school

and eventually applied to college. He failed his university entry exam—passing the math and science portions and bombing everything else. He opted to attend trade school for a year, then reapplied to the university. He was accepted after his second time taking the test.

Einstein went on to make groundbreaking advancements in physics, science, and math—including the twentieth century's most famous equation, $E=MC^2$. In layman's terms, that just means that small amounts of mass can be converted into huge amounts of energy, and serves as the basis of development of nuclear power.

Einstein's Brain

Einstein's brain continued to live on, so to speak, even after his death in 1955. Thomas Stoltz Harvey, a Princeton Hospital pathologist who conducted Einstein's autopsy, secretly removed Einstein's brain during the procedure without consent. He took the brain home and kept it in a jar, with plans of studying it. Harvey never did release this study and ended up returning the brain to Einstein's granddaughter Evelyn . . . a whopping forty-two years later! Harvey, then in his eighties, drove from New Jersey to California with the brain in the trunk of his Buick Skylark. Evelyn wasn't interested in keeping the brain, so Harvey then brought it back to Princeton University, where it currently resides.

Scientists aren't a hundred percent sure why Einstein was such a smarty-pants. His brain was actually on the smaller side of average, but denser in the areas of the brain linked with math and science. He also lacked the Sylvian fissure, which separates the brain's frontal and temporal lobes. This is thought to have improved communication between neurons in the brain.

FUN FACT:

Einstein's brain wasn't the only stolen body part. The physicist's eyeballs went to Henry Abrams, Einstein's eye doctor. Rumor has it, they are still in a safe-deposit box in New York City.

This is NOT Einstein's eyeball!

OTHER BRAINIACS

LEONARDO DA VINCI

(April 15, 1452–May 2, 1519)
A painter, inventor, sculptor, architect, musician, engineer, and scientist, Da Vinci is credited with sketching the first parachute, helicopter, airplane, tank, repeating rifle, swinging bridge, paddleboat, and motorcar. That's a lot of accomplishments for a single person—but Da Vinci had extra time on his hands. The genius adhered to a polyphasic sleep cycle—in other words, he slept multiple times a day. His daily sleep diet consisted of four thirty-minute naps, meaning the man got only two hours of shut-eye a day!

HYPATIA

(born between AD 350 and 370; died March 415)

This Greek woman was the first notable female scholar in mathematics. She taught philosophy and astronomy. It is believed that she charted many celestial bodies and invented the hydrometer, which determines the density and gravity of liquids.

STEPHEN HAWKING

(January 8, 1942–present)

Hawking is well known for his contributions to cosmology and quantum gravity, especially when it comes to black holes. He also believes that it is most mathematically probable that alien life-forms exist.

In 1963, Hawking was diagnosed with Lou Gehrig's disease. Doctors gave him two to three years to live. Though the disease's progression left him paralyzed, Hawking has gone on to live a long and amazing life. He was named a fellow of the Royal Society of London, and earned a professorial chair at Cambridge University that was once held by Sir Isaac Newton (1642–1727).

In a 2004 *New York Times* interview, Hawking was asked about his IQ rating. His answer? "I have no idea. People who boast about their IQ are losers."

MARIA GAETANA AGNESI

(May 16, 1718–January 9, 1799)

The oldest of twenty-one children, Agnesi was an Italian linguist, mathematician, and philosopher. She could speak Italian and French by the time she was five and Greek, Hebrew, Spanish, German, and Latin by thirteen.

By age fourteen, Maria Gaetana Agnesi was tackling tough problems in geometry and ballistics—the science of the flight patterns of bullets and cannonballs. This was an especially strange field of interest for a girl, especially at a time when most girls didn't receive any formal education. In fact, it was rare for a woman to even know how to read in the eighteenth century.

Agnesi taught at the University of Bologna and was the first female to be appointed as a professor. There is a crater on Venus named after her.

SRINIVASA RAMANUJAN

(December 22, 1887–April 26, 1920)

Ramanujan excelled in math but stunk at other subjects. Amazingly, this Indian mathematician, who made significant contributions to mathematics, had little formal training. In fact, he lost his college scholarship when he failed all of his nonmathematical course work.

He first encountered formal mathematics at the age of ten and demonstrated a high skill level. He was given a trigonometry book, and by the age of twelve, he discovered theorems on his own. One of his biggest contributions to mathematics is the Ramanujan conjecture. This conjecture states that the Fourier coefficients $\tau(n)$ of the cusp form $\Delta(z)$ of weight 12, defined in modular form theory, satisfy $|\tau(p)| \leq 2p^{11/2}$, when p is a prime number.

That makes perfect sense.

WILLIAM JAMES SIDIS

(April 1, 1898–July 17, 1944)

A child prodigy, Sidis could supposedly read the *New York Times* at eighteen months. He taught himself eight languages by the age of eight: Latin,

Greek, French, Russian, German, Hebrew, Turkish, and Armenian. He also invented another language called Vendergood.

Sidis was enrolled at Harvard University at the age of eleven. In 1914, he graduated with honors at the ripe old age of sixteen and became somewhat of a local celebrity.

Unlike many brainiacs, Sidis seemed to excel at a variety of subjects, including American history, cosmology, civil engineering, linguistics, and anthropology—just to name a few. The average American's IQ is about 100. It is estimated that Sidis's IQ fell somewhere between 250 and 300.

Animal Brains

GREAT APES: Scientists have taught chimpanzees, orangutans, and other great apes to communicate through American Sign Language and computer keyboards. Oddly enough, some of those apes successfully tutored other apes in the art of sign language!

WHALES AND DOLPHINS: These sea mammals create complex mental images to remember great distances. They also communicate with songs, but since they can't read, they aren't very good at karaoke.

ELEPHANTS: Pachyderms have remarkable memories (see Circus Peanuts). They also perform death rituals and grieve the loss of a family member.

PARROTS: Some parrots are capable of speaking human languages. They can initiate short conversations. One parrot, N'kisi, knows 971 English words. "Knowing" means that the bird can use a word in five or more different contexts without mimicking a human speaking. Just don't tell a parrot a secret . . . they're blabbermouths.

OCTOPI: These eight-legged creatures are equipped with large brains (compared to their body size), and often use them in mischievous ways. In captivity, octopi have been known to escape from their tanks in order to eat fish from nearby aquariums. Though they typically make a break for it when there are no witnesses, the wet trail they leave behind is a dead giveaway.

CROWS: Some consider these black birds to be a pest. However, Crows are incredibly clever. They have been known to remember human faces, build complex tools, and intuitively understand what other crows are thinking.

BODY TO BRAIN RATIO:

SPARROW 1/12

HUMAN
1/40

MOUSE
1/40

CAT
1/100

DOG
1/125

FROG
1/172

LION
1/550

ELEPHANT
1/560

HORSE
1/600

SHARK
1/2496

HIPPOPOTAMUS
1/2789

Chitlins

Chitlins, also called chitterlings, top many a table in the American South. These rubbery tubes are sautéed until crispy, chopped and stewed or battered, fried, and served with a touch of vinegar and chili sauce—which is just enough accoutrement to cover up the fact that they are pig poop chutes. Yep, a chitlin is made from none other than a pig's intestine. Trust me, they're fantastic.

The most important thing to remember when making chitlins is to clean them like crazy. You can't have any remnants of the chitlins' former life making it onto your plate. If not cleaned properly prior to cooking, chitlins can leave a nasty bitter aftertaste. Yuck. Even under the best of circumstances the chitlins will often have a deep barnyard aroma and aftertaste. You will like that part best of all once you start eating them . . . again, trust me.

Chitlins fall into the offal category. "Offal"

literally means "off fall," the stuff that falls off the animal when it's butchered. Tongue, throat, lungs, heart, liver, spleen, kidneys, uterus, intestines, and all the rest . . . If plain intestines aren't your thing, look no further than your typical sausage or hot dog. The casings are often made out of intestines, although some casings are made from digestible plastic, which, if you ask me, is *really* bizarre.

HOW TO CLEAN CHITLINS

In order to get the most flavorful chitlins, this is one step you do not want to miss. It can take a lot of time, but it's worth it.

1. Boil the chitlins for five to ten minutes.

2. Separate the membrane from the chitlins.

3. Rinse the chitlins three to four times until the

water no longer feels greasy and the water is not cloudy.

4. You've got clean chitlins, ready for use in your favorite recipe.

I like to braise them for an hour or so in seasoned water. Then drain them and sauté them in bacon fat until crispy. Season them with hot chilis and vinegar and serve them with scrambled eggs and toast. They are heavenly.

GOT SOUL?

Today, soul food is synonymous with Southern comfort food. But the origins of this culinary genre go back to the darker days of U.S. history. Slave owners would eat "good" cuts of meat, leaving their scraps for the slaves to eat. That included pig's feet, chitlins, and the rest of the offal. Meals would be supplemented with other foods slave owners felt were not good enough for the dinner table in the main house—like rice, okra, collard greens, and corn. Ironically, many of these ingredients were familiar foods to the enslaved Africans, and recipes developed around

these ingredients were lovingly passed down through generations.

Soul food is most often linked to the African-American population in the South. The name "soul food" was first attached to the cuisine in the mid-sixties, when the word "soul" was often used to describe African-American culture. For example, African-American music of that era was dubbed "soul music." Some of my favorite soul food dishes are listed on the next page. My favorite soul food restaurant is My Sisters & Me in Detroit, Michigan. Try to visit!

more SOUL

SWEET POTATO PIE: A typical Southern Thanksgiving dessert, it's a lot like pumpkin pie but made with sweet potatoes. Add a little marshmallow topping. Yum.

PEACH COBBLER: A cobbler is like a pie without a crust on the bottom. When it's made with the super-ripe and juicy peaches in the South, you can't find a tastier dessert.

SWEET TEA: In the South, you can't go far without being offered some sweet tea. It's a tea that has been specially brewed to hold as much sweetener as possible.

BISCUITS: Biscuits are soft leavened bread that look similar to a roll. They accompany pretty much anything. Don't forget loads of gravy!

GRITS: Originally a Native American dish, grits are coarsely ground-up corn kernels usually eaten for breakfast. I love mine with cheese.

BLACK-EYED PEAS: No, not like will.i.am and Fergie. Black-eyed peas are actually beans with a black mark on them that looks like little eyes. Add some chopped bacon or ham hocks (better yet, add both), onion, garlic, and hot sauce, and you've got a fantastic side dish.

COLLARD GREENS: Collard greens are large green vegetable leaves from the same family as broccoli and cabbage. It's tradition in the South to eat collard greens on New Year's Day. It is supposed to ensure wealth in the coming year since the greens look like money. Any good restaurant featuring Southern food or soul food will have plenty of collards on the menu.

OKRA: Also known as lady's fingers, okra comes from the mallow family, the same one that the original marshmallows came from. Okra is a great source of fiber if you can get past its sliminess.

POULTRY GIBLETS: Giblets are just another name for offal, but from a fowl. Think fried turkey gizzards, chicken liver, and other goodies from our feathered friends.

HOG MAW: The lining of a pig stomach, stuffed with potatoes, sausage, cabbage, and seasoning. Sounds gross but tastes delicious.

FAT BACK: Fairly straightforward—a cut of meat off the back of the pig, which is full of delicious fat. It is often made into pork rinds, or cracklings, one of my favorite snacks.

PIG'S FEET: There is no mistaking what this is. Pig's feet are fantastic little treats. The meat on the knuckle makes for good eatin'.

FRIED FISH: Fresh fish fried up until crispy. You can't go wrong with a fried catfish sandwich, served with lots of hot sauce.

INTESTINE & DIGESTION

The intestine is the longest part of the digestive tract in humans and other mammals, and it connects the stomach to the anus. Pigs' and humans' digestive tracts take the same path. Food starts at the mouth, moving through the esophagus to the stomach to the intestines to the anus. It finally ends up on the barnyard floor or in the toilet. The intestines are made up of the small intestine, which absorbs nutrients into the body; the large intestine, which absorbs water from the body; and the rectum.

Intestines are very long. A full-grown pig's large intestine can be 16 feet long, and its small intestine can reach up to 60 feet! Typically, chitlins are made from the small intestines of about a six-month-old pig, so the size of the small intestine is closer to about 54 feet. That's still a lot of chitlins.

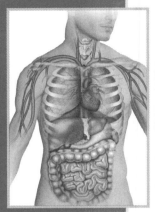

Chitlin Circuit

The Chitlin Circuit was a group of performance venues in the eastern and southern United States that were considered safe places for African-American entertainers (musicians, comedians, etc.) to perform during a time of racial segregation.

The name comes from "chitlin" because they are considered soul food, and it also plays on the term "Borscht Belt," which were venues in New York that were safe for Jewish entertainers to play at during the forties, fifties, and sixties.

FAMOUS CHITLIN CIRCUIT VENUES

Royal Peacock in Atlanta • The Cotton Club, Wilt's Smalls Paradise, and the Apollo Theater in New York • Roberts Show Lounge, Club DeLisa, and the Regal Theater in Chicago • The Howard Theatre in Washington, D.C. • The Uptown Theatre in Philadelphia • The Royal Theatre in Baltimore • The Fox Theatre in Detroit • The Victory Grill in Austin, Texas • The Hippodrome Theatre in Richmond, Virginia • The Ritz Theatre in Jacksonville, Florida

FAMOUS CHITLIN CIRCUIT PERFORMERS

Billie Holiday • Ray Charles • Duke Ellington • Ella Fitzgerald • Muddy Waters • Wilson Pickett • Ike and Tina Turner • B. B. King • Cab Calloway

Circus Peanuts

My wife loves techno-candy. I'm talking neon-colored Nerds, glow-in-the-dark sour gummy worms—basically anything that looks like it might be poisonous. My son will eat anything. Me? I'm kinda a throwback guy. Necco Wafers and I are besties, and Good & Plentys, Lemonheads or Grapeheads, Atomic FireBalls, Charms Sweet Pops, Tootsie Rolls, cigarette gum, Amish taffy, saltwater taffy, Boston Baked Beans, Bit-O-Honey, Slo Pokes, and Charleston Chews to name a few, are all frequently seen in

my carry-on bag as I traipse around the globe with my mouth wide open. For me, candy is comfort food, and no candy fits the bill for me quite like Circus Peanuts. When I am away from the family, a little sweet in the evening keeps me tethered to home, even when I am 5,000 miles away in a jungle.

When I was about five years old, I vividly remember walking into Ye' Old Penny Candy Store in Watermill, Long Island. It was raining and my mom didn't know what to do with me.

Huge mistake loading me up with sugar, but I don't judge. The ancient glass cases were filled with trays of hard candy, licorice, taffy, chocolates, chewy fruit slices, and a greatest hits of the best commercial-candy-store goodies that 1966 had to offer. I remember thinking maybe I would spend my nickel on the Nickel Nips. I loved those little wax bottles. Maybe those petite reams of white paper with the little hard-sugar colored dots laid out in neat rows? Nope. I saw the Circus Peanuts. Done deal.

Slender, orange curls of banana-scented marshmallow-ish taffy-ish peanut-ish heaven. I buy, I hold, I marvel, I eat. And for the next forty-five years, every time I open a small bag I get the same vibe. I go right back to being that kid staring at the case, my mom getting antsy as I try to decide on what I want with my worn little nickel, and realizing now, as then, that I made the right choice.

The Mysterious Origin of the Circus Peanut

What do the Pyramids of Giza, the Hanging Gardens of Babylon, and Circus Peanuts all have in common? Their beginnings are unknown; a mystery shrouded in ambiguity, wrapped in an enigma. Also, I'm pretty sure they're all banana flavored.

Hitting the market in the 1800s, Circus Peanuts are one of the oldest—and most bizarre—candies still produced today. No one really knows why they're called Circus Peanuts, why they are orange, or why they are banana flavored. They were originally a seasonal treat only available in the spring in 5- and 10-cent candy stores. After the creation of polyethylene film in the 1940s, the candies could be sold year-round.

Oddly enough, Circus Peanuts contain no peanuts, nor are they flavored like peanuts. They're a delicious mixture of sugar, pork gelatin, corn syrup, soy protein, food coloring, and artificial flavoring. Rumor has it, the weird choice to make them banana flavored stuck after a freak banana-oil accident.

According to sources from Spangler, one of the only remaining companies still making Circus Peanuts, this candy is one of the most difficult to make. They need the perfect conditions to have the correct consistency—too much moisture creates a thin, crusty deposit; too little and the peanut will cave inward. The mixture of sugars and pork gelatin must be squirted into starch molds, which take out the moisture and form the peanut shape. The next day the peanuts are crystallized in temperature-controlled rooms for twenty-four hours.

When it comes to eating Circus Peanuts, there is no correct method. Some like them factory-fresh, right out of the bag. Others go for the microwave method—nuke 'em for ten seconds and you're good to go. Then there is the delayed gratification option. Simply open the bag and let the little nuggets turn from mallow to rock solid. If you're not sure how you like your Circus Peanuts, do a blind taste test with all three.

DIDJA KNOW: ELEPHANTS

When you hear "circus," you think bearded ladies, creepy clowns piling out of tiny cars, and, of course, elephants. Contrary to popular belief, did you know that pachyderms do not like to eat peanuts? The Ringling Bros. Circus reports that their elephants eat hay, fruits, vegetables, and fresh bread. In the wild, elephants prefer grasses, plants, and fruit. Their favorite treat? Delicious tree bark.

Elephants use their trunk like an arm to eat food. They even drink using their trunks by sucking up water and blowing it into their mouths. Not sure I would want to drink anything that came spraying out my nose, but then again, I'm sure elephants wouldn't eat a lot of the stuff that I have.

An elephant never forgets.

FACT: Elephants show signs of having a superior memory compared to other animals. Elephants can remember the scent of those who have harmed them, a food source, and other elephants. Though those memories seem simple, elephants also show signs of remembering the past. Elephants grieve the loss of family members and can remember those they have lost. In studies, a family herd of elephants will show a greater response to the bones and tusks of relatives than to other objects.

Elephants are afraid of mice.

FICTION: Just like humans, some elephants have irrational fears (see page 175). Why would a massive elephant be afraid of a measly mouse? The same reason some humans are afraid of mice. While some of us would not flinch at the sight of a mouse (or the taste of one), others would run for the hills, screaming like a little girl. A mouse might startle some elephants, but the vast majority would ignore it completely.

FAMOUS CLOWNS

Not Dan Rice, but hey, this is still some impressive circus performing!

DAN RICE (1823–1900)

The most famous American pre–Civil War clown, Rice was an eloquent wordsmith whose sayings are still used widely today.

"Jump on the bandwagon"

During Zachary Taylor's campaign for president, Rice invited him to campaign on the circus bandwagon.

"One-horse show"

Rice was poor early in his career and only had one horse. Competitors made fun of him calling it a "one-horse show." Even though he had only one horse, he put on a good show.

"The greatest show on Earth"

Rice's circus was called this in an Arkansas newspaper decades before the phrase became popular among other circuses.

BOZO THE CLOWN
(1946–?)

Created by Alan W. Livingston in the mid-1940s, Bozo was originally used as a storyteller for children's read-along books. By 1949, Livingston brought the character to life on the television program *Bozo's Circus*. Unlike other programs, Bozo the Clown was created not as a syndicated show but as a franchise. Local TV stations could put on their own local productions of the show complete with their own Bozo. One of the most well-known Bozo actors was Larry Harmon. Harmon started his own animation studio, where he produced a successful Bozo cartoon series. He also took advantage of his clown celebrity to get his giant clown foot into exclusive doors. Harmon did zero-gravity flight simulations in the astronaut training plane "The Vomit Comet," ran for president in 1984, and even visited cannibals in New Guinea in his full garb. Of course none of the cannibals wanted to eat him. Word on the street: Clowns taste funny.

KRUSTY THE CLOWN
(1989–)

Krusty the Clown, born Herschel Krustofski, is the host of *The Krusty the Clown Show* on *The Simpsons*.

Originally, Krusty was made to look like Homer Simpson in clown makeup. However, the show altered his design in 1995, giving him a different-shaped mouth and perma-bags under his eyes to distinguish him from Homer. Krusty's signature raspy voice, played by Emmy Award–winning voice-over artist Dan Castellaneta, is based on WGN-TV Chicago's Bob Bell's version of Bozo the Clown.

The Simpsons' team of writers love the Krusty character as he serves as a vehicle for making showbiz jokes. In fact, many of Krusty's experiences and anecdotes come from the real lives of the writing staff.

In 2003, Krusty was included in a special history of Jewish entertainers exhibit in New York City's Jewish Museum.

Clown fish earned their name due to their brilliant orange and white stripes, but that's where the similarities to Bozo end. These creatures tend to be homebodies and stink at making balloon animals.

COCKROACHES

(Giant Hissing Ones!)

It looks creepy and it's definitely crawly, but the giant hissing cockroach is delicious. The insect is also known as the Madagascar hissing cockroach or the Madagascar beetle. As the name implies, the cockroach is native to Madagascar and can grow about two to four inches long. Although the cockroach is most often found hanging out in rotting logs, the insect is extremely hygienic.

Unlike most cockroaches, the hissing cockroach doesn't have wings. It makes up for not being able to fly with its excellent climbing skills. A hissing cockroach can actually scale smooth surfaces, like glass. Because of their not-so-pretty appearance, hissing cockroaches are popular "eat it if you dare" foods. In 2006, a man in England broke the record for eating the most hissing cockroaches in one minute: His total was 36 hissing cockroaches.

Eater be warned: Raw hissing cockroaches contain a mild neurotoxin that can numb the mouth and make it difficult to swallow. In almost every Asian country, you can find these bugs deep fried or stewed and dried, but they are mostly a novelty item, even in countries with long-standing insect-eating traditions.

What does the "Hiss" Mean?

Giant hissing cockroaches make a hissing noise by forcing air through breathing pores on their thorax and abdomen. They can make three distinct hissing sounds that mean different things:

THE DISTURBANCE HISS (ALL): "Hark! Who goes there?"

THE FEMALE-ATTRACTING HISS (MALES): "Hey there, beautiful. Do you believe in love at first sight, or should I walk by again?"

THE FIGHTING HISS (MALES): "Do you want a knuckle sandwich?"

Roasted cockroaches on the set of the *Bizarre Foods Halloween Special*. Which is it—a trick or a treat?

HOW TO ▸ Keep a Giant Hissing Cockroach as a Pet

Are cute puppies and fuzzy bunny rabbits not your thing? How about a ferocious-looking insect? Giant hissing cockroaches might look scary, but they are gentle, excellent pets. Here's what you need to know before picking up Fluffy. (That's what I'd name a cockroach if I ever got one):

CHECK IF IT'S LEGAL. In some states, you need a permit to keep cockroaches as pets. They want to make sure the cockroaches don't start as a couple of *pets* and turn into millions of *pests*. Before you bring your buddy home, make sure you get your permit.

MAKE A HOME FOR YOUR NEW FRIEND. A terrarium works best. Remember, they're excellent climbers and can easily crawl up and out of a glass box, so try coating the glass with petroleum jelly.

KEEP IT DARK. Cockroaches love the dark. Put logs and leaves in the terrarium to give your cockroach a place to hide.

GIVE 'EM SOME GRUB. Cockroaches enjoy foods like fresh vegetables or dry dog food, which is high in protein.

CAN COCKROACHES *REALLY* SURVIVE A NUCLEAR HOLOCAUST?

Cockroaches are tough critters. They can live a month without food, a week without water, and some cockroaches can even go without air for 45 minutes. Despite their ability to keep living through harsh conditions, eventually, they will need food, water, and air. The biggest threat to the survival of cockroaches in a nuclear holocaust is the radiation. The lethal dose of radiation to cockroaches is six to 15 times higher than to humans, but cockroaches are not the most "radiation-resistant" animals. Could cockroaches survive a nuclear holocaust? It's not likely. If the radiation doesn't get them, it will be a lack of food and water that does them in, for sure.

FUN FACTS ABOUT COCKROACHES!

- There are about 4,500 species of cockroach, but only four species are best known for being pests.

- Cockroaches typically live in a warm climate. It's the reason some cockroaches like to hang out in a house. It's nice and warm, and there is plenty of food. Don't worry though, for most species of cockroach, the house still isn't warm enough.

- Want to get rid of the cockroaches crawling in the kitchen? Turn on the light. Most cockroaches are nocturnal and will run the moment you flick the switch. Asian cockroaches, on the other hand, are attracted to light.

- It's easy to tell the difference between male and female roaches. Males sport impressive horns, which they use much in the same way as other horned animals. Male roaches will fight with one another, ramming their horns into each other until one "wins." The dominant roach will hiss more than the loser, which is thought to notify other roaches who's the boss.

- Madagascar hissing cockroaches aren't pests on the verge of overrunning your home. Instead, they mostly live on forest floors amongst the leaves, dirt, and logs. At night, they scavenge for fruit and plants.

MICHAEL BOHDAN

By daylight, Michael Bohdan is a cockroach hunter. As the proprietor of the Pest Shop, a pest control company, Michael will rid your home of roaches, termites, even armadillos. As a pest expert, he's appeared on shows like *The Tonight Show with Johnny Carson* and *Good Morning America*, and authored the book *What's Buggin' You? Michael Bohdan's Guide to Home Pest Control*.

But at night, his feelings toward the critter seem to change. Michael runs the Cockroach Hall of Fame, in Plano, Texas, where he displays dead cockroaches dressed as celebrities, as well as some roaches that are very much alive. Michael explains how his profession became his passion.

*Turn the page for more on Bohdan's roach obsession.

When did you become interested in insects?

As a child, I was always interested in bugs. I remember finding mosquito larvae swimming in a pool of standing water and thought I had discovered something fantastic.

You work in pest control during the day, but keep a museum dedicated to the insect at night. What's your *real* stance on cockroaches?

It is a love/hate relationship. In the morning, I get paid to eradicate roaches, and in the afternoon, I love to show off live and dressed-up roaches to visitors.

You've appeared on many television programs showing off bugs. When you're picking insects to show off, what is your bug of choice?

My bug of choice are the large Madagascar hissing roaches. Easy to handle, large, and people freak out when seeing them.

What inspired the museum? What was your first exhibit?

I have done some of the dressed-up roaches, but most of them were done by women I met when I traveled the U.S. They were paid $1,000 for the best-dressed roach in their city. The first exhibit, I believe, was Marilyn Monroach.

Liberoachi: the most flamboyant pest in the west!

Kicking back on the beach, roach style!

What's your newest roach addition?

I am currently working on the dancing Ellen Degenaroach, and hope to get on her show with this one.

Which cockroach exhibit is your favorite?

Liberoachi and Ross Peroach.

What intrigues you about cockroaches?

Cockroaches have been around for over 350 million years. I believe we can learn from them. In life, I have been a survivor to get where I am now. No one has helped me along the way.

Any other roach activities you enjoy?

I love to do roach races. The best one was on *Hour Magazine* in L.A. and to the sound of the "William Tell Overture." The three of us urged the roaches on with flyswatters. No roaches killed during the filming of this.

What is the most bizarre thing you've ever eaten? Have you ever eaten a giant hissing cockroach?

I have eaten some strange things like barbecue-flavored larvae of a beetle, but *not* a roach. I don't like the green-colored guts. Thanks, but no thanks.

For more information on Michael Bohdan and his Cockroach Hall of Fame, visit *www.pestshop.com*.

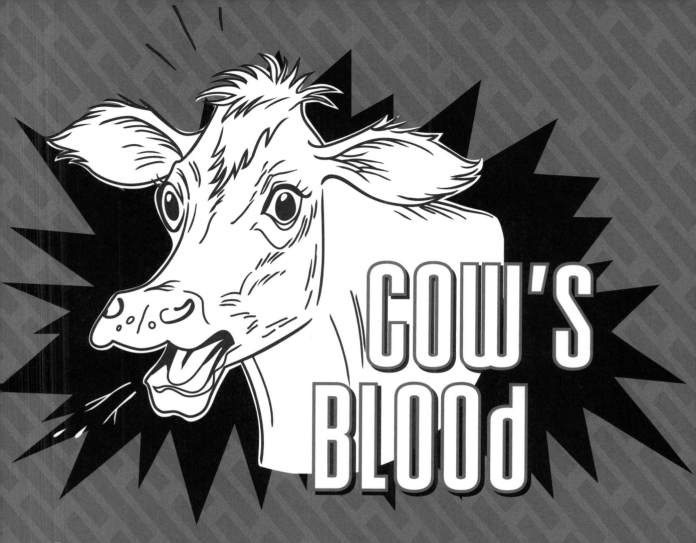

COW'S BLOOd

In many cultures, blood consumption plays an important role in a healthy lifestyle. Enthusiasts say the red stuff keeps you strong, and can even warm you up on a cool day. Chug a glass of blood and your body temperature will indeed rise a few degrees—seriously! Overcoming the psychological hurdles (not to mention the flavor) can make drinking blood challenging. Downing a glass is akin to sucking on a freshly used and discarded bandage, multiplied by a factor of a thousand.

I love super-fresh cow's blood. Sure, the first time you drink it, it's off-putting. Most people have only tasted blood after cutting a finger and then instinctively sticking it in their mouths (is this smart? I don't know!). However, blood has its nuances: There is a big difference between snake, duck, lamb, and cow's blood. The flavor changes depending on how fresh it is, and if you're drinking it straight up or not. For me, it's no longer the stuff of horror films; it's just another ingredient. Very rich in protein, with great minerally flavor, I enjoy a glass of fresh cow's blood in the same, mundane way that I enjoy something more ordinary, like a tomato.

Cow's blood is the breakfast of champions for members of the Tanzanian Masai tribe. The cow is a revered animal in Masai culture. They are a pastoral people and the act of bleeding the animal is not taken lightly. The blood is harvested from the cow as it's standing in the corrals each morning. A group of Masai will restrain the cow while one member shoots an arrow into the animal's jugular artery at a short range. The arrow has a large ring secured just aft of the arrowhead so the projectile doesn't penetrate the animal deeply. The nick is large enough to easily allow for blood collection in a liter-sized jug made out of a dried gourd called a calabash. Instead of letting the cow bleed any more than is necessary, they smear dirt mixed with the animal's own feces on and into the wound to help seal it back up. According to the Masai I met, a cow can give blood about once a month without harm to its health.

After the blood is collected, it can be consumed in a few ways. You can drink the blood, fresh and warm from the cow's body heat, or you can stir the blood and wait for it to clot on the end of the swizzle stick. The clotted blood forms a mass that can be eaten, and the removal of the blood solids allows for easy drinking later on throughout the day. Another option is to mix the blood with either curdled or fresh milk for a "blood milk shake." The combination of phosphorus, calcium, iron, hemoglobin, and hematocrit (aka red blood cells) can replenish the body in a way that few foods can. Masai women drink

My Masai guide, Edward Ngobei, shows me how to chug fresh cow's blood. It tasted like a Band-Aid, in a good way!

blood after giving birth, which can replenish any vitamins lost during labor. The Masai men will often drink blood after hunting, but when I lived with them, it was consumed for breakfast and lunch along with a dollop of curdled milk and millet porridge. Thankfully, dinner with the Masai is all about stuffing yourself on grilled beef, lamb, and goat until you pass out from overeating. It's pretty sweet.

THE MASAI PEOPLE

The Masai people are native to Kenya and northern Tanzania. The tribe reveres cows, believing God gave them the responsibility of caring for cows on Earth. For a man in the Masai community, respect is gained by the number of children and cows you have.

Other Uses for Cow's Blood

In addition to drinking it plain, cow's blood is used as an ingredient in many other cultures. You can find it in blood sausage, black pudding, and blood soup. You can eat it cured and salted. It's also used as a thickener for sauces. Besides eating it, here are some other uses for cow's blood:

GLUE: Glue made from cow's blood is often used to make plywood.

FERTILIZER: Sometimes dried cow's blood is used to feed plants.

HAIR DYE: In ancient Persia, women would dye their hair using coloring made from hyena's, tadpole's, and cow's blood.

TABOO FOODS: This is the grub that people do not consume for cultural, religious, or hygienic reasons. In the Judaic tradition, it is not kosher to consume the blood of an animal because it is considered the "life of the animal." All meat must be salted to absorb and remove blood before consumption. Jehovah's Witnesses prohibit the consumption of blood, including blood transfusions. Highly observant Muslims and Jews alike don't eat pork.

How Now, Brown Cow?

- A cow weighs about 1,000 pounds and has 4.376 gallons of blood.

- A cow typically spends six to seven hours a day eating.

- Cows chew about fifty times per minute.

- A cow has more than 40,000 jaw movements per day.

- Cows drink 35 gallons of water a day.

- Cows do not bite grass; they curl their tongue around it and pick it.

- Cows have one stomach with four digestive compartments.

- Cows are able to climb up stairs, but not down. They cannot bend their knees properly to descend.

BLOODY MOVIES

f blood makes you squirm, you're going to want to stay away from these flicks. They're some of the bloodiest out there:

PSYCHO (1960): After a young woman steals $40,000 from her employer, she runs away and makes a stop at the Bates Motel. Turns out the motel owner, Norman Bates, and his "mother" are not too fond of strangers. In the famous shower scene when Marion Crane, played by Janet Leigh, is murdered, blood runs down the drain. The blood is actually chocolate syrup, which shows up better than stage blood on black-and-white film.

CARRIE (1976): Carrie is a timid, unpopular high school student with telekinetic powers. As a joke, bullies rig the prom election that crowns Carrie as queen. Her initial excitement quickly switches to rage when her jerky peers dump a bucket of pig's blood on her. She, in turn, flies off the handle in an insane fit of telekinetic rage. When filming the prom scene, Sissy Spacek, who plays Carrie, was covered in stage blood. The blood would quickly dry under the lights and Spacek had to be hosed down between takes to clean off the dried blood.

DRACULA (1931): Count Dracula moves to London and stalks a young woman who looks delicious. Okay, this isn't a very bloody movie, but they sure do talk about blood a lot. If you get a chance to see the film, keep an eye out for the huge rats. They're actually played by opossums and armadillos.

RESERVOIR DOGS (1992): A rainbow of characters star in this grim story of a diamond heist gone awry. When the film was shot, a real paramedic was kept on the set to make sure that after Mr. Orange (played by Tim Roth) took a bullet in the gut, he lost a realistic amount of blood. Roth would lie in the fake blood for so long that it would dry to the floor and have to be scraped off the ground.

DIY BLOOD

Making your own scary movie? Here's how to make some realistic-looking stage blood:

- ¼ cup of creamy peanut butter
- 1 pint of thick white corn syrup
- ¼ cup dishwashing soap (warm colors work best)
- ¼ oz. red food coloring
- 5 drops of blue food coloring

1. Take 1/2 cup of corn syrup and stir it with the peanut butter until it is runny.

2. Add dishwashing soap and red food coloring.

3. Add the rest of the corn syrup.

4. Add drops of blue food coloring until you get the perfect blood color.

PROTHEMOL

Prothemol is a food alternative made primarily from cow's blood and is used to feed many malnourished children. It's a mixture of cow's blood plasma, dried egg white, vitamin A, and wheat flour. It's yellowish and odorless, and it's put into food or a sweetened beverage and dissolved, adding the nutrients needed for a healthy diet directly into the food itself. Gross, but very much necessary in our world today.

crayfish

Lobster, crab, and shrimp are all crustaceans. These briny, intense oceanic treats fetch big dough in fancy restaurants. Also called crawdads and crawfish, crayfish, on the other hand, are kind of like the black sheep of the crustacean family. Perhaps it's because they look a lot like bugs (in fact, all crustaceans and insects are relative species) and carry a less-than-appetizing stigma. Perhaps because some are saltwater species and others fresh water? Freshwater crays can be awfully muddy-tasting and the few available saltwater species are fragile in the extreme and can taste ammoniated after just the briefest of trips to your table.

There are more than 400 different crayfish species, of which 250 live in the United States. I've always considered Louisiana to be crayfish headquarters, so if you want to try some of the world's best, go there. The red swamp crawfish and the white-river crawfish are the most popular choices. The crawdads are typically boiled with a seasoning of salt, cayenne pepper, lemon, garlic, and bay leaves, but every cook has their own favorite "boil" spices, and I think you should always toss in some other stewy items, like carrots, onions, potatoes, and corn. Anyway, you boil your water, add your vegetables and seasoning, cook for a few minutes, add your crayfish, cook for six minutes or so until done, toss a load of ice into the pot to drop the temperature and force the spices into the crays, drain, and serve. Then pick one up, twist off the head, and suck the brain, organs, and bits of meat out from the crayfish's head and body. Split the tail and eat that too. Of course, there's more than one way to eat a crayfish. You can pick the meat out of its tiny body, or if you're really adventurous (or a seal) you can eat the critters whole. Lean, and with as much protein as a T-bone steak, crayfish are good eatin'.

There are lots of ways to cook a crayfish. Here's a dish that includes hot dogs!

YOUR NOSE KNOWS!

When it comes to seafood, especially shellfish, the fresher the better. Seafood that isn't fresh will reek of a pungent, chemical aroma. This ammoniated stench is the byproduct of bacteria breaking down proteins in the animal's body. I dare you to leave a crawfish out on the counter overnight, and then take a whiff. It smells like an institution. I can't quite put my finger on it—does it reek of a prison or a hospital? Maybe it's a public school. Sometimes, I think it's cat pee. In any case, I don't like eating seafood that stings my nose with its chemical scent. It's foul!

HOW TO ▶ SUCK THE HEAD OF A CRAYFISH

The head of the crayfish contains an organ called the hepatopancreas—the animal's main energy storage spot. The local lingo for this rich, yellow substance is the "fat," and you'd be crazy to skip it. Locals suggest you rip off the head and suck out the fat, but you could also dig it out with your finger. Messy hands and lots of slurping are perfectly acceptable etiquette.

CRAYFISH GO BY MANY NAMES

crawdad • crayfish • crawdaddy • rock lobster • ecrevisse • spiny lobster • sea crawfish • mudbugs • yabbies • lobster • crawfish • crawcrab • crabs • bugs • ditchbug • nipper • raki • panzerkrebs • langoustine • homard • cangrejo de río • camaron • shaitanbalyk • astaci • zarigani • acocil • chraebs • crowfish • crays • freshwater lobster • freshwater crab • mud puppy • spoondogs • craws • crawlfish • ditchbug • grave diggers • rivierkreeften

crayfish around the world

Louisiana is traditionally a hot spot for crayfish, but these delicious little buggers are on menus across the globe:

SCANDINAVIA: Popular in Sweden and Finland, crayfish are typically boiled and flavored with salt, sugar, ale, and the flowers of a dill plant. The dish is usually served cold during August, the fishing season.

FRANCE: Crayfish is common in French cuisine. Heads-up, if a dish has *à la Nantua* at the end of it, it typically means it is made with a crayfish.

SPAIN: Crayfish is called *cangrejo de río* or "river crab" in Spanish. Stewed in a tomato sauce, crayfish is a delicacy served during the fishing season.

MEXICO: Crayfish is called "acocil" in Mexico, and it's an important part of pre-colonial Aztec cuisine. Usually, it's boiled and seasoned.

NIGERIA: Crayfish are called "the core of Nigerian cooking." The crustacean is sun dried or smoked.

CHINA: Crayfish did not become popular in China until the late 1990s. Now it is typically steamed and flavored Mala style, a numbing hot Sichuan pepper and hot chili combo.

HOW TO ▶ Catch a Crayfish

Most crayfish live in slow-moving fresh water, so head to a lake, pond, or creek. Place a net (a towel works too) in the water and cover it with sand. Put some bait on the net to entice the crayfish. Crayfish will eat almost anything, but the professionals swear anything from meat to cat food to fresh, oily fish will work. When the crayfish walk on the towel or net, lift it up.

Be very careful of the crayfish's claws. If you get pinched, it hurts like heck. If the crayfish latches onto you with its claw, place your hand in the water and relax your muscles. The crayfish should let go. To avoid any pinching mishaps, only pick up a crayfish by its midsection.

MORE FUN FACTS ABOUT CRAYFISH

- Crayfish are a small cousin to lobster. They are typically found eating animals (both living and dead) and plants in freshwater lakes, ponds, and creeks.

- They have a hard exterior shell called an exoskeleton. They have no bones because their exoskeleton protects and holds all of their innards. Around late June, crayfish will shed their shells. They usually eat the newly molted shell for the calcium.

- When crayfish crawl they move forward, but they swim in a backwards motion. If a crayfish loses its leg or claw, it will grow back.

- On average, crayfish are about 7 inches long.

- Male crayfish often fight with female crayfish in order to mate. The males usually lose a limb.

- An egg-carrying female crayfish is said to be "in berry" because the group of crayfish eggs looks similar to a berry.

- Lots of crayfish is an indication of a healthy body of water. If the population is thriving, chances are the ecosystem is in good shape. If there aren't any crayfish to speak of, think twice before jumping in.

Mardi Gras

Every year between Ash Wednesday and Easter, it is Christian tradition to observe Lent. During the period of forty days and forty nights, Christians give up certain foods and vice. Mardi Gras translates to "Fat Tuesday" in French. It refers to the day before Lent where people eat rich, fatty foods and party like crazy before they begin the forty days' fast. New Orleans, Louisiana, is famous (and infamous) for its Mardi Gras celebrations. People of all religions dress up for parades, attend masquerade balls, eat like pigs, and drink like fish. General debauchery ensues. In general, it's a rip-roaring time for all who attend.

One of the most beloved traditions in the Mardi Gras celebration is the king cake. This colorful cake is decorated in purple, green, and gold, and is said to represent justice, faith, and power. Each king cake has a small trinket placed inside it before frosting. Usually it is a small plastic baby, representing the baby Jesus. You can also use an almond or any other small trinket. As tradition has it, the person who eats the slice with the trinket inside brings the next cake. Just try not to choke on the plastic baby.

EMERIL'S KING CAKE

Emeril Lagasse coined the cooking phrases "kick it up a notch!" and "bam!" He's also one of the most-beloved and highly regarded chefs in the world. Here's his go-to recipe for the Mardi Gras king cake.

Makes 20 to 22 servings

2 envelopes active dry yeast
¼ cup granulated sugar
1 cup warm milk (about 110°F)
12 tablespoons (1½ sticks) unsalted butter, melted
5 large egg yolks, at room temperature
5 cups bleached all-purpose flour
2 teaspoons salt
1 teaspoon freshly grated nutmeg

1 teaspoon finely grated lemon zest
1 teaspoon vegetable oil
1 pound cream cheese, at room temperature
4 cups confectioners' sugar
1 plastic king cake baby or a pecan half
5 tablespoons milk, at room temperature
3 tablespoons fresh lemon juice
Purple-, green-, and gold-tinted sugar sprinkles

- Combine the yeast, granulated sugar, and warm milk in the bowl of an electric stand mixer. Beat at low speed with the whisk attachment for 30 seconds, then turn mixer off and allow the mixture to sit until foamy, about 10 minutes. Add the melted butter and the egg yolks to the milk and whip quickly to incorporate. Replace the whisk attachment with the dough hook. Add the flour, salt, nutmeg, and lemon zest to the mixer and beat until everything is incorporated. Increase the speed to high and beat until the dough pulls away from the sides of the bowl, forms a ball, and starts to climb up the dough hook.

- Remove the dough from the bowl. Using your hands, form the dough into a smooth ball. Lightly oil a medium bowl with the vegetable oil. Place the dough in the oiled bowl and turn it to oil all sides. Cover with plastic wrap and set aside in a warm, draft-free place until doubled in size, about 2 hours.

- Meanwhile, make the filling. In a large mixing bowl, combine the cream cheese and 1 cup of the confectioners' sugar. Blend by hand or with an electric mixer on low speed. Set aside.

- Line a large (12-by-17-inch) baking sheet with parchment paper.

- Turn the dough out onto a lightly floured work surface. Using your fingers, pat it out into a rectangle about 30 inches long and 6 inches wide.

- Spread the filling evenly along one of the long sides of the dough. Fold the other long edge over so that the long edges meet. Seal the dough on all edges by pinching the dough together. Finally, bring the two ends (of what should now be a long, filled cylinder of dough) together, and pinch the ends together to form a ring. Place the filled dough onto the prepared baking sheet, seam side down. Insert the king cake baby or pecan half into the ring from the bottom so that it is completely hidden by the dough.

- Cover the ring with plastic wrap or a clean kitchen towel and place in a warm, draft-free place. Let the dough rise until doubled in size, about 45 minutes.

- Meanwhile, preheat the oven to 350°F.

- Brush the top of the risen dough with 2 tablespoons of the milk. Bake until golden brown, 25 to 30 minutes. Remove from the oven and let cool completely on a wire rack.

- Make the icing. Combine the remaining 3 tablespoons milk, the lemon juice, and the remaining 3 cups confectioners' sugar in medium mixing bowl. Stir to blend well. With a rubber spatula, spread the icing evenly over the top of the cake (or drizzle, as desired). Sprinkle with the sugar crystals, alternating colors around the cake.

- The cake is traditionally cut into 2-inch-thick slices and served to all guests in attendance. The person whose piece contains the hidden plastic baby is crowned "king for a day" and is considered responsible for holding the next king cake party.

CUY (Guinea Pig)

My son was four years old and just wrapping up another year of preschool when Daddy came to visit the class. I walked in and a little girl began screaming, "Don't eat Simon! He's going to eat Simon!!! . . . AAARRGGGHHH!"

Well, I didn't. This teeny little rodent we lovingly keep as pets populates many a classroom. I don't get it. They make lousy companions (have you ever seen one fetch?!), and despite the mythology that they are good starter pets here in the United States, in the Andes Mountains,

they're called *almuerzo*. That's Spanish for "lunch."

Guinea pig farming dates back to 5000 BC, and it's still a very profitable livestock in Peru, Bolivia, and some parts of Ecuador and Colombia. Cuy, as they are called in South America, take up little space, reproduce quickly, and are high in protein and low in fat and cholesterol. Peruvians are especially fond of cuy, and eat nearly 65 million of them per year. Guinea pigs provide 50 percent of all animal protein consumed in Peru. I know, I know: It seems really weird to eat a guinea pig. However, all it takes is one piping-hot bite of roasted cuy to realize they're just as delicious as they are cute and cuddly.

I love a roasted cuy, but you can also find it fried or boiled. It tastes a lot like rabbit—a little richer and gamier than chicken—but with the mouth feel of roasted pork shoulder. Much like live lobster, some restaurants allow patrons to select their dinner from a crate of live guinea pigs. For the best eatin', go for a younger pig: Their skin crisps up nicely compared to their older counterparts, who tend to carry more rubbery fat between their skin and muscle. Once your meal is served, ditch the fork and knife. This delicacy is meant to be eaten with your hands. Be warned—cuy will leave a sweet and smoky stench on your hands that can be tough to get rid

First, we roast the cuy. Then, we duel! (Just kidding. We just ate them. Also, try to avoid eating the teeth!)

of. The locals call the scent *tufo*. Don't wash up too soon. I recommend walking around reeking of *tufo*—it will give you some serious street cred with the locals.

Weird Guinea Pig Facts

- Guinea pigs are a type of rodent that originated in the Andes. They do not exist naturally in the wild.

- Guinea pigs have been commonly kept as pets in Western society ever since they were traded to Europeans in the sixteenth century.

- Guinea pigs startle easily. When startled they will either freeze for a long period of time or run for cover. In large groups, guinea pigs will stampede to confuse predators.

- When guinea pigs get excited they will repeatedly hop in the air. This is called "popcorning." Butter and salt not included.

Guinea Pig RX

Traditional folk healers called *curanderos* are fairly common in Latin America. Highly respected in their community, a *curandero* can supposedly heal his patients using a combination of Catholic elements (like holy water) and rituals from indigenous cultures that are believed to have healing powers.

One of those elements is a guinea pig, which is used to diagnose diseases like jaundice, rheumatism, arthritis, and typhus. Black guinea pigs are considered the best for this purpose. Guinea pigs can be used as a treatment and are rubbed against the body of a patient in a bizarre cleansing ritual. Sometimes guinea pigs are cut open so *curanderos* may examine their guts to further support their diagnosis.

Testing, Testing 1-2-3

Historically, guinea pigs were commonly used as test subjects in scientific experiments. Thus, the term "guinea pig" (meaning "someone/something that is used as a test subject") was coined. These days, it's mostly mice and rats who serve as guinea pigs.

HOW TO PREPARE CUY

This recipe is not for the faint of heart!

> 3 or 4 cuys
> ½ cup of ground toasted corn, or cornmeal
> 4 pounds of parboiled potatoes, cut into slices
> 8 cloves of garlic
> 6 fresh hot peppers, either red or yellow
> ½ cup oil
> ½ cup water
> salt, pepper, and cumin to taste

- Skin the cuys in hot water, remove internal organs, and clean in salted water.

- Rub the cuys with a mix of the pepper, salt, and cumin.

- Skewer over a barbecue.

- Prepare a sauce with the oil, peppers, garlic, and cornmeal with the water from the potatoes or broth. Cook a few minutes until the peppers are cooked.

- When tender, place the meat in a serving dish and spoon the sauce over it. Serve with the boiled potatoes.

Tests We Don't Want to Be the Guinea Pig For

1. What happens when human beings are sucked into a black hole?

2. What are the physical and mental ramifications of riding "It's a Small World" for forty-eight consecutive hours?

3. Could a smelly elevator fart make you go blind?

4. How many sloppy Joes are just too many?

5. First-ever human brain transplant.

Dancing Shrimp

A few years back I journeyed to Isaan, in Thailand, to shoot an episode of *Bizarre Foods*. Most of the food we ate was scary (even by my standards!), but one meal was memorable for a variety of reasons. Mostly because I ate one of the weirdest foods I had ever tried (dung beetles, see page 58), and dined on one of my favorite foods, a Thai shrimp salad made with live shrimp.

This is a dish I had never been able to taste in the place it comes from, the small farms that dot this spectacular region of Thailand. Isaan sits in the northeast corner of the country, located on the Khorat Plateau, and is bordered by the Mekong River (along the border with Laos) to the north and east, and by Cambodia to the southeast. Isaan is the poorest area of the country. The average per capita income is about $400 per year and 70 percent of the population is classified as poor. Originally forced by poverty to be creative in finding edible protein, the people of the region famously eat a wide variety of

Dancing shrimp served in Thailand. The key is to eat the shrimp before it jumps off your plate!

creatures, such as lizards, frogs, and fried insects such as grasshoppers, crickets, silkworms, and as I mentioned before, dung beetles.

My crew and I were way out in the countryside when we finally found the farm we were looking for. Our hosts were a grandmother, her daughters, and her grandkids. We rolled up our pant legs and headed down to the river. Wading in, we all lined up, several feet apart, nets in hand, and started marching upstream, dipping our nets as we went, pulling shrimp out by the dozens with each dip. Trust me, I wasn't getting as many as Grandma and the girls, but I wanted to fill my bucket as best I could because I wanted to contribute to our meal of Kung Den. That's what they call the salad made of small, fresh, live shrimp, lemongrass, fish sauce, lime, tomato, basil, toasted rice powder, and fresh hot chiles. It's the acid from the lime that makes the shrimp "dance" in the bowl . . . and in your mouth!

I had two big problems: First, when we sat down I took too many shrimp, so my bowl was filled too high, which meant that I was constantly cleaning up my eating area as the shrimp dove again and again out of the bowl. This also meant I was doing more tidying than eating. Let me tell you, this is not good, particularly with a dish this supremely excellent. The flavors are perfect together, especially with the lemongrass-chile–rice powder troika playing loudest in the band, one of my favorite of all the Thai tastes. After a few minutes, the shrimp danced less, the sun finally sank, the air cooled off, and Grandma stopped yelling at me. I was eating in a rhythm now, wadding up balls of sticky rice and pulling delicious piles of shrimp and sauce out of my bowl, which Grandma had now taken to refilling. A word of warning: This dish is spicy, but you also need to be an aggressive chewer to make sure you stop the shrimp from wriggling around and using its shell and carapace to stab your cheeks and gums. Good teeth trump dancing shrimp every time, which is why moms all over the world make sure their kids brush their teeth twice a day.

Shrimp Cocktail

No American steakhouse menu is complete without a classic shrimp cocktail—cold, cooked shrimp served with a spicy tomato and horseradish sauce. Though this dish originated at the turn of the twentieth century, it wasn't until the 1920s that it truly gained popularity. Cocktail foods (such as shrimp and fruit cocktails) gained traction during Prohibition, a time when alcoholic cocktails were banned in the United States. Not only were these kinds of nonalcoholic "cocktails" the perfect way to kick off a meal, but they were also a creative way to utilize stemware.

ANGELS ON HORSEBACK:
Sounds like the name of a Top 40 girl band, but this is in fact an appetizer made of oysters wrapped with bacon. Angels on horseback originated in the United Kingdom, but you can find them on many an American menu (sometimes called pigs in a blanket). For all you anti-shellfish people, opt for an order of Devils on Horseback, which swaps out the oysters for dates.

OYSTERS ROCKEFELLER:
Named after gazillionaire John D. Rockefeller, this appetizer originated at Antoine's Restaurant in New Orleans in 1899. An extremely rich dish (hence the nod to Rockefeller), oysters on the half shell are topped with various other ingredients (often spinach or parsley, cheese, a rich butter sauce, and bread crumbs), then baked or broiled.

DEVILED EGGS:
Though deviled eggs are commonplace in the United States, ancient Romans enjoyed some form of a hard-boiled egg topped with a spicy sauce. The classic recipe you've probably encountered uses a halved hard-boiled egg. Mayonnaise and mustard are blended with the yolks, then spooned back into the cup of the hard egg white. The eggs are sprinkled with paprika.

ESCARGOT:
Butter and garlic can make shoe leather taste delicious. In the case of escargot, this rich culinary combo makes a sluggish snail wow the pants off diners. Often served as a starter, snails are plucked from their shells, gutted, cooked in butter, garlic, and parsley, then placed back in the shells for a decadent treat.

TO DEVEIN OR NOT TO DEVEIN?
Ever notice the dark string that runs down the back of a shrimp? It's called the vein, and no, it's not filled with blood. It's a shrimp's digestive tract, intestine, poop chute, whatever you want to call it. A lot of people prefer to remove it, but it's safe to eat if cooked properly. Just prepare yourself for the possibility of a gritty explosion of earthy flavor.

DANCING FOR THE REST OF US: A TIMELINE

FOX-TROT (1914)

It's not a fox, nor a trot, but your great-grandma was probably into it.

CHARLESTON (1923)

This dance move accompanied the 1920s flapper craze, with gutsy women occasionally flashing their—*gasp!*—knees to male onlookers.

LINDY HOP (1927)

Named after Charles Lindbergh, aka the first guy to fly solo across the Atlantic, the Lindy Hop was later popularized in forties swing dancing.

DANCE MARATHON (1930)

A Depression-era fad, dancing for hours on end may sound fun, but it's rather torturous in practice. The longest-lasting marathon? From August 29, 1930, through April 1, 1931, **Mike Ritof** and **Edith Boudreaux** danced for 5,154 hours, 48 minutes, or 214 days.

COLLEGIATE SHAG (1937)

This series of hops and taps has nothing to do with shag carpet, shag haircuts, or *Austin Powers: The Spy Who Shagged Me.*

BUNNY HOP (1953)

A conga-line dance that's decidedly more fun if you happen to file in behind your crush (and not big Auntie Bertha).

THE TWIST (1960)

Made famous by Chubby Checker, the Twist looks less like a dance and more like a mime drying off his butt with a bath towel while squishing a bug with his foot . . . but hey, we still love it.

MASHED POTATO (1962)

Your favorite side dish just go funky. It's sort of a pigeon-toed take on the Twist, and it was much more popular than the 1963 spin-off dance, the Gravy Boat.

THE HUSTLE (1975)

The Hustle became an international dance craze after the release of Van McCoy and the Soul City Symphony's song of the same name. Oddly enough, this ditty sounds more like elevator music than something you cut a rug to, but let it slide. Disco was weird in general.

"Y.M.C.A." (1978)

Spelling quiz or dance move? Either way, every post-1978 wedding, bar mitzvah, and homecoming dance is obligated to play it.

MOONWALK (1983)

Cab Calloway did a mean moonwalk in the 1930s, but Michael Jackson's catapulted the break-dancing step into pop culture phenomena in the "Billie Jean" music video.

"SUPER BOWL SHUFFLE" (1985)

NFL players singing and dancing? You'd have to be as big as a linebacker to pull this one off.

"WALK LIKE AN EGYPTIAN" (1987)

1380 BC meets AD 1980s with this Bangles hit song and dance moves. For a quick tutorial, mix poses seen in ancient hieroglyphs with the huge, overly permed mall hair of the 1980s.

"THE HUMPTY DANCE" (1990)

If you like to rhyme, like your beats funky, you're spunky, and I like your oatmeal lumpy, you'll love "The Humpty Dance."

"ACHY BREAKY HEART" (1992)

Back before he was Miley's dad, Billy Ray Cyrus was just a mullet-headed hick with a broken heart and one-hit-wonder dance song.

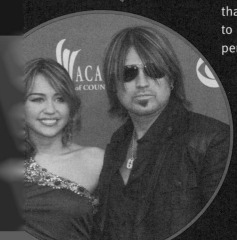

"MACARENA" (1995)

Not sure what's worse—doing this dance or getting the song stuck in your head.

"CHA-CHA SLIDE" (2000)

Perfect for those with two left feet, the "Cha-Cha Slide" is basically a list of instructions. Just follow the idiot-proof song lyrics and you're good to go.

"CUPID SHUFFLE" (2007)

The "Cha-Cha Slide's" younger sibling, here's yet another step-by-step line dance that's so easy, your grandma could do it.

FLASH MOB (2009)

A "spontaneous" choreographed group dance that pops up in the most unexpected of places. Grocery stores, department stores, and malls are common settings, but the most famous flash mob, staged in Chicago for the final season of *The Oprah Winfrey Show*, involved more than 20,000 people dancing to a live Black Eyed Peas performance.

OXYMORONS:

a combination of *contradictory* or incongruous words (such as *jumbo shrimp*); *broadly*: something (as a concept) that is made up of contradictory or incongruous elements.

CRUEL KINDNESS

AIRLINE FOOD

HEAD BUTT

LAMP SHADE

VIRTUAL REALITY

KNOWN SECRET

EXTREMELY AVERAGE

GOLD SILVERWARE

GRADUATE STUDENT

ACT NATURALLY

DONKEY

From their big teeth to their stringy tails, for Americans, there is not one thing about a donkey that looks appetizing. Historically, donkeys and their meat haven't earned a great reputation for much more than their work ethic. In ancient Athens, only the poor would stoop to eating such a thing. And at the turn of the nineteenth century, a Maltese food shortage caused starving residents to consume the protein out of necessity. Turns out, the people of Malta had the same reaction as me: Donkey is actually pretty good.

So where does one go to find this hee-hawing delicacy? Namibia and Nigeria boast thriving donkey-meat markets, but the meat is often passed off as beef to non-locals. Chalk it up to a Western aversion to donkey meat. If you want to find a culture unashamed of their love of donkey meat, head to Italy, where the Sardinians grill a mean burro and the Venetians make a donkey salami that is one of my top-ten all-time favorite foods. All that aside, true donkey-dining devotees place China at the top of the list. An ancient Chinese proverb says, "Dragon meat in the sky and donkey meat on the earth." This more or less means there is no such thing as dragon meat (unless you know something I don't), so the next best thing is donkey. You can find donkey-meat sandwiches all over Beijing, and for the pinnacle of donkey-dining experiences, try Beijing Qun Sheng Shi Jia Can Yin, a restaurant devoted to all things ass.

This Beijing, China, restaurant specializes in donkey meat. Inviting friends means you can order more grub. Bring it on!

Aside from flavor, there are a lot of reasons to eat donkey. The meat is high in protein and low in fat. In traditional Chinese medicine, the donkey's skin, called *ejiao*, will supposedly make the consumer's skin more beautiful. Did I mention it also tastes delicious?

Sliced thin and stir fried, it's one of the great wok-tossed dishes of the world. Ditto braised donkey hot pots, cold roasted donkey loin sliced thin and served with pickled vegetables—I am telling you, this stuff is amazing and tastes like an earthier version of veal. In a world in desperate need of lean, healthy alternative proteins, and for a meat whose popularity might ease the toxic strain on the meat and poultry industries, I think it's time for carnivores to try this amazingly delicious "other" red meat.

Jack Facts

- Jacks (male donkeys) and jennies (female donkeys) have been "hitting the road" and lugging our loads since about 3000 BC, when they were first domesticated by humans.

- Adapted to desert lands, donkeys spend fourteen to sixteen hours per day looking for food, but they only eat about 1.5 percent of their body weight.

- "Donkey" comes from the word "dun," meaning dull grayish-brown, the color of a donkey.

- Within their fifty-year life span, these stubborn creatures will live solo until they choose to mate.

- Donkeys usually give birth to a single foal. Multiple births are very rare.

- Though they might look depressed and bored, asses are real butt-kickers. They use a powerful hind-kick and a strong bite to defend themselves.

- Because donkeys live so far from one another, they have developed a way to communicate. Donkeys make a sound called a bray, which can be heard up to 3 kilometers away! When a donkey has something to say, it will make a loud "hee-haw" noise for about twenty seconds.

- Donkeys make great pets. They are kind, loving, and loyal. Plus, they have great smiles.

CAST YOUR VOTE

In the United States, the two largest political parties are often represented by animals. The Republicans have the elephant and the Democrats have the donkey. The symbols originated in political cartoons drawn by Thomas Nast for *Harper's Weekly*. Although the Democrats proudly wear the donkey as their symbol, it was first used as an insult. On January 15, 1870, the liberal symbol first appeared kicking a dead lion. It was a commentary on the Democratic press abusing the memory of Edwin M. Stanton, Lincoln's former secretary of war, who had died suddenly. The cartoon read, "A live jackass kicking a dead lion," a play on words from the proverb, "a live ass is better than a dead lion."

The elephant made its debut three days after the Democrats had won the majority of the House of Representatives on November 7, 1874. As a Republican, Nast jabbed at his fellow Republicans, depicting them as an elephant running from the Democratic *New York Herald*, symbolized by the donkey.

Surprisingly, rats, snakes, dogs, platypuses, fire ants, and hairy-nosed wombats haven't been adopted as the official animal of any political party.

DONKEY VS. MULE

Donkeys are part of the Equidae family, which includes horses and zebras. Since they are closely related species, they are still able to reproduce. This means a male donkey and a female horse can have a baby. The offspring of this pairing is called a mule. If the donkey is the baby mama and the horse is the father, they produce a hinny.

DUNG BEETLES

Dung beetles live in, eat, and breathe poop. Okay, they don't breathe it, but I'll bet they wish they could. They hang around big animals until they find a steaming pile of dung, which they'll dive into like it's Thanksgiving dinner. Literally.

The poop-eating scavenger is a popular snack in rural Laos and Thailand. In fact, dung beetles are so popular that in some villages, people will "reserve" a dung pile in communal grazing areas by marking it with a sign. The dung beetles found within are then off-limits. It's the bug-eating equivalent of marking your lobster traps with colorful buoys.

If you want to harvest dung beetles in tropical climes, follow your nose just before sunset. When you reach the stinky dung pile—and it has to be fresh enough to be soft, and old enough (a few hours) to have attracted the beetles—grab a sturdy stick and dig around until you find dinner. Once a dung pile is picked clean, the beetles are thrown into a bucket of water. Much to my surprise, I learned this is not done to clean them. Ironically, no one who eats them cares that they have been recently extracted from a giant cow pie! The bath simply waterlogs the wings so the dung beetle can't fly away. The bucket sits for a few hours or overnight, supposedly allowing the dung beetles to expel any dung they've ingested. The next day, they're tossed into a clean bucket of water to soak for a couple hours. Trim their wings and legs off before cooking, then toss in a wok with oil, basil, chiles, and lemongrass until they're nice and crispy. Before you shove a bunch in your mouth, be *sure* the cook has removed the legs and wings. If not, you should do so—that way they won't get stuck in your throat. Ack!

In Thailand, they soak dung beetles in water not to clean them, but to keep them from flying away!

Eat . . . Feces!

- The majority of a dung beetle's diet consists of feces. For a change of flavor, they will sometimes eat mushrooms or decaying leaves and fruit.

- Also called scarab beetles, there are about 7,000 different species of them around the world.

- There are three types of dung beetles, categorized by how they act around dung. There are:

ROLLERS, who roll dung into spherical balls. They will eat the dung balls or use them as brooding chambers.

TUNNELERS, who dig holes into dung piles and bury themselves.

DWELLERS, who live in manure, but they do not roll or tunnel.

- Dung beetles will live in any habitat dung can be found: desert, farmland, forest, and grassland. They prefer moderate temperatures and can be found on every continent except Antarctica.

- Dung beetles aren't picky eaters. They will eat all types of dung, but they prefer dung from herbivores.

- Dung beetles have an excellent sense of smell that will lead them to their next meal. Others hang on to an animal until it relieves itself and then they eat the waste. Some stay near the animal's rear end and just eat the "leftovers" on their fur.

- Dung beetles don't need to drink water, because they get all of the H_2O needed from dung.

- Dung beetles help clean. Because dung beetles remove feces and bury it, they are very helpful in agriculture. They help put more nutrients into the soil and keep it soft, as well as clean up the piles of poop. They also clean up after themselves by eating their own dung.

- Burrowing owls will collect the waste of other animals and spread it around their nests. The dung acts as bait for the dung beetles as the owls can eat them up as the beetles try to find the dung.

Hieroglyphics

| A | B | C | D | E | F | G | H | I | J | K | L | M | N | O | P | Q | R | S | T | U | V | W | X | Y | Z |

Ancient Egyptians believed that dung beetles, or scarabs, kept the Earth revolving like a large ball of dung. Today, scarab charms are often worn for good luck in Egypt. The scarab symbol, 🪲, was used in hieroglyphics to mean "to transform" or "to become," most likely due to their life cycle, changing from an egg to larva to a dung beetle.

Hieroglyphics was a writing system developed by ancient Egyptians that uses pictures as letters and as words. The symbols cover the pyramids and ancient runes in Egypt, telling stories and giving warnings to those trying to enter sacred tombs. The hieroglyphic alphabet is above. See if you can decode the punch line to this knee slapper:

A dung beetle walks into a bar.
"Pardon me," he says to the bartender.

" _ ?"

(Answer: "Is this stool taken?")

OTHER ANIMALS THAT CALL **POOP** DINNER

PENGUINS. You know, those adorable little waddling black-and-white birds? A hungry penguin will peck its way through frozen guano looking for small leftovers of crustaceans, like krill. The mommy and daddy penguins will take it a step further by regurgitating the poop bits for their babies to eat. Yum!

FLIES. Flies are frequent fliers and pee-ers. They pee every few minutes. That means they need to drink a lot of water to keep up. And the fly's favorite source of water? A big, juicy turd. Flies don't have tongues or teeth. Their mouths are like sponges, so they can only eat liquids. After they're done sponging up water from a heap of poop, they might head for a solid food. In order to turn the food to liquid, flies will vomit up chemicals to break down foods before they go in their mouths.

MAGGOTS. Although not all maggots enjoy the taste of poop (some are vegetarians), there are those that love to chow down on cow pie. They also enjoy decomposing garbage, sewage, and rotting flesh.

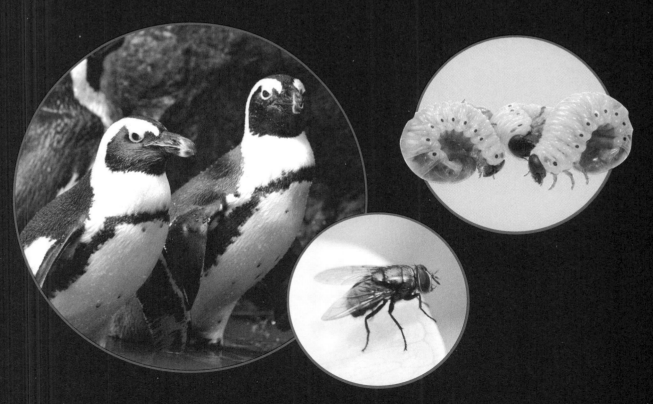

DURIAN

Is it a fart? Limburger cheese? Funky garbage fumes? Rotted onions? The sock laundry bag after a high school basketball tourney? No, that smell could simply be fresh fruit.

Durian, known in Asia as the "king of fruits," is crowned with a spiky exterior and filled with flesh stinking of old wet underwear. This fruit from the durian tree is a popular snack in Southeast Asia, so popular that when the fruit is at its peak in Malaysia, the whole country literally shuts down to get this foul-smelling and horrendously flavored fruit. So be warned: It is not for the faint of heart.

Durian is native to Brunei, Indonesia, and Malaysia. Harvesters gather the fruit in the summer months. The fruit is more or less the size and weight of a bowling ball, and covered in spikes. Durian farmers string out nets under the trees, allowing the death-bombs to collect safely above the ground. People often say durian have eyes because they tend to fall at night when there are less people around. In Indonesia, the saying, *Ketiban durian runtuh* translates to "getting a fallen durian," meaning getting struck with unexpected luck.

The large fruit is covered with 2-inch greenish-brown thorns that can pierce the skin if you're not careful. It's like nature made this fruit come with its own built-in warning. The fruit's flesh emits a smell so strong it goes through the inch-thick husk. Animals can smell the fruit from a half-mile away. It's even banned from many hotels, taxis, buses, elevators, stores, and ferries in the countries where it's most popular. Don't even try to get it on a plane. Now why would they do that if it were so tasty? Exactly. You do the math.

I've eaten durian about fifteen times, and I just don't like it. I don't like its taste or its mouth feel. But if you can get past the threatening exterior and the harsh smell, you might end up loving

Durian smells like dirty socks, tastes like rotten onions, and its putrid gases linger in your belly and mouth for a day. And you wonder why I don't like it!

the fruit. It's traditionally eaten plain or as a flavoring in a variety of sweets: durian ice cream, durian biscuits, and durian cake.

Humans aren't the only ones who worship the fruit; deer, pigs, squirrels, elephants, orangutans, and even tigers love to find a lone durian waiting to be eaten.

HOW TO SERVE THE FRUIT:

Feeling gutsy? Great. Here's how you attack a durian:

- Hold with heavy gloves or towel with stem end facing away from you.

- Slice through it top to bottom on one of the thorn growth lines and split it apart.

- Scoop one of the lobes surrounding the seeds out with your fingers or a spoon.

- To neutralize the bad-breath smell after eating the fruit, fill the empty shell with salt water and scratch your fingernails on the inside of the shell. The shell contains a chemical that neutralizes the scent of the fruit. Put the scrapings from the shell in your mouth and swish around.

A Fruit That's NOT Good For You?

NO DURIANS!

Even though it's a fruit, durian doesn't necessarily do the body good. It can cause excessive sweating, raise your blood pressure, and should be avoided altogether if you're pregnant. According to a study by the University of Tsukuba in Japan, the sulfur in the fruit can inhibit the body's ability to clear away toxins in other foods and in your body by 70 percent. This means it is very dangerous to consume the fruit with medications, alcohol, or even the caffeine in coffee and soda.

Bizarre Architecture (Durian-Inspired?!)

In Singapore, the Esplanade Building houses a concert hall, recital rooms, and studios. The outside of the building gave the building its name among the locals: the durian. It's domed with hundreds of spiky structures jutting from the roof.

OTHER STRUCTURES THAT MIGHT HAVE YOU THINKING YOU'RE LOOKING AT SOMETHING ELSE

The Baha'i faith has built only seven houses of worship worldwide. The Baha'i House of Worship in New Delhi, commonly referred to as the Lotus Temple, is recognized as a masterpiece of twentieth-century architecture.

This giant picnic basket is the home office of Longaberger, manufacturer of . . . baskets!

Built for the World's Fair in 1958, the Atomium was made to look like a molecule. The spheres contain exhibition halls, a restaurant, and more, all connected by escalators. (Brussels, Belgium)

Other Smelly Foods

POPCORN: Just try making popcorn without someone asking you, "Did someone make popcorn?" Impossible.

SURSTRÖMMING: Fermenting herring. Let the dry heaving commence!

100-YEAR EGG: An egg packed with tea water, clay, lime, ash, and salt, then rolled in rice hulls. If that's not smelly enough, the egg is then left to sit for three years. It tastes like cheese, very stinky cheese.

ANY SORT OF FISH PRODUCT in the microwave. Unless you live with seals, no one will appreciate that lingering scent.

FiSH HEaD CuRRY

Finally, an assertive soup that isn't afraid to look you right in the eyes! Fish head curry consists of fish head (or heads) stewed in curry, coconut milk, and traditional curry seasoning. Some cooks in Singapore, where the dish is commonly found, make it this way in an Indian style. Others add plenty of Kafir lime to create a more Thai-style dish. Either way, they're both delicious and stocked with all sorts of veggies.

The dish seems so odd you'd expect it to be deeply embedded in tradition, but in fact the dish is a bizarre food newbie, said to have originated in Singapore in the mid-twentieth century. The story goes like this: An Indian chef noticed his Chinese customers liked fish heads, so he created a dish just for them by simply adding fish heads to his curry.

In Singapore and Malaysia, the dish is made with red snapper, stewed in Kerala-style curry with okra and eggplant. You'll typically find it with rice or bread served on the side. Red snapper is no longer available in Singapore, so it must be imported for the dish. The eyes, lips, cheeks, collars, and the bones/cartilage of the head itself all have unique individual tastes and make the soup very rich with the collagen found in this delicious part of the snapper.

Syncretic Dishes . . . HUH?

Fish head curry is a syncretic dish, which means people associate it with a different cuisine than to the cuisine it really belongs. Many cultures claim fish head curry as their own, but the dish belongs to the cuisine of Singapore. Here are some other syncretic dishes:

GENERAL TSO'S CHICKEN & SESAME CHICKEN:
You order General Tso's chicken at a Chinese restaurant thinking it came from China, but the dish originated in the United States, made by Chinese chefs who came here in the great Chinese culinary diaspora of the seventies.

CHICKEN TIKKA MASALA: This dish is often associated with India, but it was actually created by Indian chefs in London.

HAMBURGER: As American as hamburgers seem, they did not originate in the United States. Hamburgers got their name from Hamburg, Germany, owing to the cultural makeup of the first cooks who made the little sliders so popular in this country. Minced beef on bread had been around Europe since the fifteenth century.

FOIE GRAS: Foie gras is a French delicacy, but the dish got its beginnings, long before the French got a hold of it, in ancient Egypt.

Waiter, there's a fish head in my soup! Just kidding, it's just a typical lunch in Singapore.

CURRY

In Western cultures, curry is a generic description for spiced dishes, usually a soup or a stew, from Indian and South Asian countries. "Curry" comes from the Tamil word *kari,* which means "sauce, cooked vegetables, and meat." Curry doesn't necessarily have curry powder in it. Curry powder is a mixture of different spices that will vary depending on the cuisine. Most recipes for curry powder are made from coriander, turmeric, cumin, fenugreek, and red pepper.

Delish Fish (Heads)

The red snapper gets its name from its brilliant red skin and its snapping teeth. These fish swim in the western Atlantic Ocean. On average, they weigh about four to six pounds and have soft and tender meat.

The best red snappers have clear, bright red eyes. Buy the fish with the skin still on. It holds the fish together and the red scales show you are buying real red snapper, not some lame poser fish.

Q: What do you call a fish with no eyes?
A: A fshhhhhhhhhh

Other fish heads that make for good eating

1. Tempura-fried shrimp heads
2. Smelt fries (you eat the whole fish in two bites—head, scales, tail, and all!)
3. Salmon cheeks
4. Crayfish (see page 40)

Table Manners around the World

In the United States, it is rude to eat with your hands. In other places, it's customary. Table manners are different around the world. In India it is only acceptable to eat with the right hand. The left hand is traditionally used to wipe your nether regions after using the bathroom, and therefore, disgusting to eat with. Here are some other table manners to keep in mind, if you're eating around the globe:

TANZANIA

It's rude to turn up early for dinner. Aim for a few minutes late. Do not show the sole of your foot to other diners. Avoid touching your face while eating.

AFGHANISTAN

Guests are seated farthest from the door and are expected to eat the most. "Did you get enough? Do you want more? Eat! Eat! You're all skin and bones! EAT!" A polite host will coax their guests to eat more. So help them out by having a second (or third) helping.

CHINA

Diners usually sit at a round or square table. The eldest or most important person will sit farthest from the door. If you're using chopsticks, use them with your right hand between the thumb and first two fingers.

When the chopsticks are not in use, place

them next to each other with both ends touching. Don't lay them across your plate or bowl. Worse still, don't stick them in your rice bowl poking up. That simulates some traditional gravesite markings in Asian culture and is the ultimate form of disrespect.

Don't clean your plate! That signifies to your host that you're still hungry and didn't get enough to eat.

JAPAN

Don't dive right into your food. You must wait for the host to tell you to eat three times before starting. It is acceptable—even desirable—to make a slurping sound when eating hot noodles. There is no tipping in Japanese restaurants in Japan. Of course, you should still tip in a Japanese restaurant in the United States. Do not stick your chopsticks vertically into a bowl of food—it's considered bad luck. The only place it's acceptable to do this is at a Japanese funeral, where placing a bowl of rice with vertical chopsticks on the altar is part of the ritual.

PHILIPPINES

The head of the household or the guest of honor sits at the head of the table. Never place your elbows on the table. Wait for the host to tell you where to sit.

BRAZIL

Wash your hands each time before going to the table. Avoid digging in with your hands—cutlery is always used.

CHILE

Before you pour a drink for yourself, first offer to pour a drink for your neighbors. Earn your membership in the clean plate club—it's poor form to leave a scrap of food on the plate.

FRANCE

French bread is often torn rather than cut. Once you're finished, place your cutlery vertically on your plate. This indicates to a waiter that you are finished with your meal. Never, ever, ever-ever-ever ask for "le ketchup." To a French chef, it's akin to telling them their dish tastes like dog food.

SWITZERLAND

To toast in Switzerland, hold up your glass and look into everyone's eyes before drinking. Always keep both hands above the table.

RUSSIA

Small food should not be cut. Tell the chef the meal was good before leaving the table (if the chef is eating with you).

POLAND

If you order fish in Poland, don't ever flip the filet to the other side. Superstition says that this will cause the fishing boat it came from to capsize. True or just an old wives' tale? I'm not sure, but I wouldn't want to be responsible for that!

SPAIN

Garbage-schmarbage. In Spain's numerous tapas bars, it's customary to throw shrimp shells, napkins, toothpicks, crumbs, and other trash right onto the floor.

CANADA

A satisfying belch will alert the chef or host that you really enjoyed the meal.

FUGU

Beware of Japanese restaurants boasting glowing, globular, fish-shaped lanterns. . . . It might mean a meal there could be your last. The lantern signifies that they specialize in serving toxic fugu, also called puffer fish or blowfish. Japan has been home to the fugu dish for hundreds of years, if not more. Anthropologists discovered remnants of fugu meals dating back more than 2,300 years.

The dish has been banned several times throughout the country's history. A Japanese emperor feared being poisoned by the fish, so he banned it for his own safety. It's no wonder why—people died left and right from consuming the delicacy. In 1958, the Japanese government nipped this problem in the fins with the development of the fugu chef training and licensing process. It begins with a two- to three-year apprenticeship where novitiates learn all about the fish and how to cut it. Hopefully they pay attention to the other details that will ensure that you live through their meals when they graduate. Still, an estimated twenty diners still die each year after eating fugu.

When raw, fugu has a very mild, melon-cucumber flavor, with the texture of cooked lettuce and is almost flavorless in taste. So why, you ask, would people still eat it sashimi style? It's all about the thrill. A full fugu-coursed tasting meal is another thing entirely. Smoked "tea" made from the roasted fins arrives like a soup course and is insanely aromatic. Tempura of fugu is sweet and textured like baby catfish, firm to the bite and melting when chewed. Fugu is not always consumed raw and is ideally eaten in a restaurant that offers many different preparations of the dish. It's not scary to eat, but I wouldn't buy fugu at the local gas station restaurant.

Puffer Fish

Don't mess with a puffer fish. These swift swimmers will unleash some serious wrath if provoked. If the fish can't make a quick getaway (they're capable of sudden bursts of speed if they sense danger), the fugu will fill their bellies with water and air. The fish blows up like a balloon, expelling the pointy spines that cover its body into a predator's body, mouth, or if it's too late, throat. If the fugu is indeed ingested, it still gets the last laugh. Whatever eats the blowfish will feel peachy for a while but will eventually die from the toxins released by the fish.

Six Ways to Eat Fugu

1. SASHIMI: The most common way to serve fugu. It is often called *fugu sashi* or *tessa*. The fugu is sliced into small, so-thin-they're-transparent slices.

2. MILT: The soft roe of the blowfish is often grilled and served with salt.

3. FRIED: So much for deep-fried chicken, how about some deep-fried fugu called *fugu Kara-age*?

4. BAKED: The fins of the fugu are dried out, baked, and served with a glass of hot sake.

5. STEW: *Fugu-chiri* is fugu with simmered vegetables.

6. SALAD: *Yubiki* is a salad served with the skin of the fugu. Before you bite into this, make sure all of the spikes have been removed. Ouch!

POISON CONTROL

Fugu has eleven body parts that are so poisonous, one bite could send you to your grave. The most poisonous parts of the fish are the liver, ovaries, and skin. The liver is so strong, it's illegal to sell it in Japan.

Though it's rare, people do die from fugu poisoning. Think you might have fugu poisoning? Look for these symptoms, and if you experience any, seek treatment immediately:

- Paralysis of the mouth, including the tongue and lips. This typically occurs when eating fugu since some of the toxin is still present in the meat.

- Hyper-salivation, sweating, headache, weakness, tremors, and eventually total loss of muscle function.

- Paralysis of the diaphragm, which blocks oxygen and leads to asphyxiation.

If you can survive the first twenty-four hours of the poisoning, you'll most likely recover with no residual effects over the next few days. Prior to heart-monitoring machines, the Japanese waited three days before burying someone with fugu poisoning in case they were still alive but had no way to communicate it to anyone.

FUGU FARMING

Think floating cages. Fugu are usually harvested in the spring during spawning season. They are best eaten in the fall and winter because they fatten up to stay warm. You can buy fugu in grocery stores precut, but it's illegal to sell whole fugu to the public. A benefit to farming is creating nearly poison-free fugu. The fish aren't born with much poison in their bodies. They eat bacteria that contain the toxin and build up an immunity over time. Fugu farmers have found that if they don't let the fish eat the bacteria, they can produce safe fugu. But where is the fun in eating that, I ask you?

FUN WITH FUGU

Hey, kids, don't try this at home. Fugu chefs use different-colored trays to separate the poisoned meat from the edible meat. Black means it's good to eat; red means danger. The whole process involves roughly thirty steps, and takes about twenty minutes.

THINGS ON THE BLACK TRAY:
Mouth, pectoral and dorsal fins, tail, side skin from gill to tail.

THINGS ON THE RED TRAY:
Gills, ovaries, gonads, heart, liver, kidneys, gall bladder, eyes, and intestines.

Other Foods that Might KILL YOU

BOODOG

This meal is made from marmot, a large mountain rodent. Marmots frequently carry the bubonic plague in their bloodstream. From approximately 1348 to 1500, the plague took out nearly two-thirds of the world's population. (See page 146 for more on the Black Death.) I passed on trying this dish in Mongolia—it didn't look very safe to eat.

RHUBARB

Rhubarb is a tricky one. It's delicious in pie and cake (well, I think so, anyway), but that is only the stems. Rhubarb leaves contain oxalic acid, which can poison the body and make you very sick. But in order to get a lethal dose, you'd have to eat 11 pounds of rhubarb leaves!

MUSHROOMS

While many mushrooms are completely safe to eat, some are just plain deadly. The death cap mushroom looks almost identical to the perfectly edible straw mushroom. If you don't know what type of mushroom you've eaten, you'll quickly find out since the death cap will cause immediate liver and kidney damage, leading to untimely death.

SAN-NAKJI

Also known as the dish "live octopus," the long, chewy, and writhing tentacles can easily get stuck in your throat and asphyxiate you.

OTHER PUFFY THINGS:

DIZZY GILLESPIE: Legendary jazz trumpeter. ➡

SEAN "PUFFY" COMBS: Entrepreneur.

POWDER-PUFF FOOTBALL: For girls only.

H.R. PUFNSTUF: Old-school TV character. Kinda creepy. ➡

"PUFF THE MAGIC DRAGON": Beloved children's song.

JERRY SEINFELD'S PUFFY SHIRT: Look it up. Would *you* wear it?!

Garlic Ice Cream

Ice cream? Weird? Wild? Let's take care of the ground rules. Ice cream is a quintessentially frozen dessert treat made with dairy products. You love it. I love it. In the United States, ice cream refers to a specific type of product, differentiated from ice milk or other frozen treats. In other countries, ice cream is *any* frozen treat like frozen custard, frozen yogurt, sorbet, and gelato. Here in America, it takes an average of fifty licks to finish a single scoop of ice cream, unless you are my son, Noah. He's a three-lick-per-scoop kind of kid. How he does it, I don't know.

These are the glory days of the American scoop-shop renaissance and chefs love to play around with the awesome canvas of an ice-cream base. It's the perfect vehicle for unusual flavors. Some good, some bad. At Humphry Slocombe in San Francisco; Scoops in L.A.; Prince Pückler's in Eugene, Oregon; and Izzy's Ice

Cream Café in St. Paul—to name a few of my favorites—you can trust any flavor in the case. But please don't ever eat garlic ice cream. I have eaten this horrible stuff and I want to spare you the pain and agony. Like smoked salmon fudge ripple ice cream, it is just wrong. Garlic ice cream is not a typical ice cream. It is savory instead of sweet.

I have eaten the stuff in Gilroy, California,

Roasted Garlic Almond Chip ice cream at Sebastian Joe's in Minneapolis. The almond and chocolate make your first lick sweet, but the garlic stands up and salutes on the back end. It's like dinner and dessert, all rolled into one!

at their famous garlic festival and in Lares, Puerto Rico, at a small scoop shop there named Heladería de Lares that is globally famous for their unusual panoply of flavors. They even have rice and beans ice cream, or roasted chicken ice cream. I am serious.

I know bad ice cream when I taste it, and I've tasted a lot of it. In the Philippines, I tried cheese-flavored ice cream on a hamburger bun. In Alaska, I ate something called Eskimo ice cream, which technically is not an ice cream at all. It's *akutaq*, made from fat, usually rendered animal lard to which dried or fresh fish (white fish or salmon) and any available fruits, like berries, are added. The high content of fat is supposed to keep the eater warm during long spells spent outdoors on the Alaskan tundra. In Japan, I tried octopus ice cream, snake ice cream, and tongue ice cream. They're all awful in their own way, but if put together in one monstrous bowl, they don't come close to the horrors of garlic ice cream. Why? Maybe it's just personal. I am not a big garlic guy to begin with, but like black pepper, it's a flavor agent that makes other things good, not something good in and of itself. And unlike a nice joint of lamb roasted in the oven, garlic doesn't make ice cream better. It makes it worse.

On the plus side of the bizarre ice-cream-flavor equation, I ate amazing artichoke gelato in Cerdo, Italy. I devoured sumptuous lick-the-machine bacon ice cream made by the masterful David Lebovitz; prosciutto, foie gras, tobacco, blood, and a gazillion other savory bizarre ice creams and loved them all . . . but that garlic ice cream is just awful. So please, consider yourself forewarned.

GILROY GARLIC FEST FACTS

Gilroy, California, is the self-proclaimed "garlic capital of the world." Gilroy holds a garlic festival every year featuring—you guessed it—garlic in multiple recipes, including bread, chicken, shrimp, sauces, popcorn, and of course, ice cream.

Think you might like garlic ice cream? Whip up a batch of your own! Here's the recipe for Gilroy Garlic Ice Cream:

GILROY GARLIC ICE CREAM

Makes 1 quart

2 cups whole milk
1 clove garlic, minced
1 vanilla bean, split in half, and the seeds
scraped out and reserved
1 cup heavy cream
1 ½ cups granulated sugar
8 egg yolks

1. Put milk, garlic, vanilla pod, and seeds in a saucepan. Bring to a boil over medium heat and remove immediately.

2. In mixing bowl, whisk the cream, sugar, and egg yolks until combined. Whisking constantly, slowly strain the hot milk mixture into the egg and sugar mixture.

3. Return the mixture to the pan and stir continuously over low heat until it thickens slightly and coats the back of a spoon, about 10–12 minutes. Do not boil!

4. Pour in a bowl and chill over an ice bath. Pour into ice-cream machine and churn until done. Freeze until ready to serve.

Other Bizarre Ice Cream Flavors

SWEET CORN ICE CREAM: Served at Gray's Ice Cream in Tiverton, Rhode Island.

GRILLED IDAHO POTATO ICE CREAM: According to a recipe from the Idaho Potato Commission, the ice cream should be served with milk chocolate cake and bacon toffee.

SAUERKRAUT ICE CREAM: Created by the women of the Scappoose, Oregon, Lions Club. In 2000, they served more than 23 gallons of this ice cream at the Scappoose Sauerkraut Festival.

BACON ICE CREAM
LOBSTER ICE CREAM

SHRIMP ICE CREAM
FISH ICE CREAM
CRAB ICE CREAM

HISTORY OF ICE CREAM

PRE-ICE CREAM

- Around approximately 3000 BC the Chinese develop the first frozen dessert by flavoring ice with fruit juice, milk, or sugar. To eat the dessert in the summer, snow and ice would need to be gathered during the winter and kept underground to keep it cold.

- Between AD 64 and 54, Roman emperor Nero has runners travel 400 kilometers to collect snow from the Apennines and bring it back to be flavored with honey and wine.

- In the late thirteenth century, Marco Polo brings the Chinese ice cream to Italy. (This is debated among historians, as it is unverifiable.)

THE ICE-CREAM ERA

- 1672: The term "ice cream" first appears in a document from the court of Charles II of England.

- Ice-cream recipes show up in England and the United States in the eighteenth century.

- 1776: The first ice-cream shop opens in the United States in New York City.

- During the colonial era, ice cream grows in popularity in the United States. Benjamin Franklin, George Washington, and Thomas Jefferson are known to be fans of ice cream.

- First Lady Dolly Madison, wife of President James Madison, serves ice cream at the inaugural ball in 1813.

- Augustus Jackson, an African American confectioner and White House chef during the 1820s, develops multiple recipes for different flavors of ice cream. He also develops the first superior technique of producing ice cream.

- In 1843, a Philadelphia woman named Nancy Johnson is given the first patent for the small, hand-cranked ice-cream freezer. This increases the popularity of ice cream.

- 1851: Commercial production of ice cream begins in the United States by a Maryland man named Jacob Fussell.

- 1905: David Strickler of Latrobe, Pennsylvania, creates the banana split.

1913: The modern freezer (direct expansion freezer) is invented. Ice cream used to be a luxurious treat because it was complicated to make without modern refrigeration.

- 1923: The first Popsicle is created by Frank Epperson in a lemon flavor. The treat is originally called an "Epsicle," but the name is changed because Epperson's children called it a Popsicle.

- Ice is cut from frozen water (lakes, ponds, etc.) and is stored underground. The ice is kept cool until it can be made into a hot summer's day treat.

THE ICE CREAM WE KNOW TODAY

Ice cream reached the level of popularity it enjoys today with the development of cheap refrigeration in the second half of the twentieth century.

What's the Difference?

There are two ice-cream types:

PHILADELPHIA STYLE: Made without eggs.

FRENCH (OR CUSTARD): Made with a custard base of egg yolks cooked with milk and cream.

SORBET: Made of sugar, water, and flavoring ingredients, most often it does not have fat.

GRANITA: Like a sorbet, but it is made by freezing the mixture in a pan instead of being churned. This is called "still freezing." It is stirred periodically to break up large ice crystals.

SHERBET: Made with dairy products, but less fatty than ice cream. Typically it is fruit flavored.

FROZEN YOGURT: Exactly how it sounds, frozen yogurt with flavoring.

PARFAITS: In France, these are desserts made from layers of different-flavored frozen custards. In the United States, parfaits are served like a sundae.

SEMIFREDDOS: Translates to "half frozen" in Italian. These are still-frozen ice creams.

FROZEN CUSTARD: Similar to French ice cream.

GELATO: From Italy, this cold dessert contains less fat and sugar, and is made with less air. Gelato can be cream- or non-cream based.

Brain Freeze

If you've ever chugged a slushy or eaten ice cream too fast, you've probably experienced a cold-stimulus headache. Commonly called a brain freeze, this painful and annoying headache occurs when cold food touches the roof of one's mouth, or the palate. The brain sends rapid messages to the head that constrict blood vessels. The brain believes the pain is coming from the nose and forehead, not the roof of the mouth. So, that's where the ice-cream headache hits you.

HOW DO YOU STOP A BRAIN FREEZE?

1. Eat slower—this will let your mouth get used to the cold and will not cause a rapid constriction.

2. Press your tongue to the roof of your mouth. Your tongue will warm up your palate and reduce swelling in your blood vessels.

garlic Facts

- April nineteenth is National Garlic Day.

- Garlic helps to reduce plaque buildup in one's arteries and lowers cholesterol levels.

- Garlic is said to keep vampires and evil spirits away.

- In ancient Greece and Rome, brides used to have bouquets of garlic and other herbs instead of flowers.

- When garlic is eaten, its cells are broken down into enzymes that contain sulfur. The enzymes are metabolized and create allyl methyl sulfide. Allyl methyl sulfide cannot be digested, so it is passed through the blood. To get rid of it, the body releases the allyl methyl sulfide through the skin in sweat and through the lungs, which explains why people get such bad garlic breath. They are actually breathing out parts of the garlic.

Giant Fruit Bats

It's a bird! It's a plane! No, it's Megabat and Flying Fox! They sound like comic-book super-heroes, but they're just a couple of the names for the large Samoan giant fruit bat. With a six-foot wing span, it's the most appropriately named animal since the toy poodle. The bats are native to the tropics of Asia, Australia, Indonesia, islands of East Africa, and the Indian and Pacific oceans, but I tried them first on the uninhabited island of Nu'utele in Samoan atoll. We hunted them at dusk, watching them wheel and spill out of a mountaintop cave, making a beeline for a nighttime feeding frenzy on the breadfruit orchard where I was staked out with half a dozen members of a local hunting club. We harvested a dozen bats pretty quickly, roasting them whole over a coconut-husk fire, drizzling them with fresh ginger juice (ginger grows everywhere on the island), and devouring them with true gusto. They were amazing.

You might think bats would taste gamey and greasy, but in the case of the giant Samoan fruit bat, this couldn't be further from the truth. These creatures only feast on fresh fruit, and unlike some other bats, they don't live in squalor. They are such clean animals that you don't even have to remove the pluck (the innards) to eat them. These taste like a mild duck, and are fantastic roasted over an open fire with fresh ginger juice. My mouth is watering. How 'bout yours?

The giant fruit bat is the largest of the fruit bat, or pteropus, family. The big pteropus family dates back to 35 million years ago. The bats are most often prepared by removing their hair and cooking pieces of the meat in a ground oven.

Giant fruit bat meat is a rare treat since in many countries the bats are protected due to overharvesting for human consumption.

You do have to be careful when eating giant fruit bat. Not only is it illegal in many places because of endangerment, but the bats are known to carry some diseases. Avoid eating bats that behave abnormally or fly in the daylight—they might have rabies. In Guam, a popular spot for fruit bat soup, the bats eat cycad plant seeds, which contain a neurotoxin. Although fruit bat is delicious, be aware that it can be dangerous.

A flying fox (aka giant fruit bat) hunted on Nu'utele Island, about 2 kilometers off the coast of Samoa.
That's an impressive wingspan!

Bat Facts

- Vampire bats are real and they stick together. The bats can go only two days without consuming blood. If a bat cannot find food, it will "beg" another bat until it shares its food . . . by regurgitating some blood for the hungry bat. That's some twisted stuff.

- Bats account for a quarter of mammals on Earth and are the only mammals who can truly fly.

- Giant fruit bats have "fruit" in their name for a reason. They love to eat fruit. They fly toward the fruit and crash into it, grabbing the food with one of their hind feet or with their clawed thumbs on their wings.

- When bats grip with their feet, their muscles are in a relaxed state. They are using their muscles when they open their feet.

- Blind as a bat? Bats are actually not blind. They have large eyes so they can see in the dark. Giant fruit bats use their excellent sense of smell to find food. Unlike other bats and swiftlets (see page 10), they do not use echolocation.

FAMOUS BLOODSUCKERS

Bats get a bad rap for being dirty, scary bloodsuckers, and some of them indeed are. Don't worry, though, it's likely the only bat you'll ever encounter is a regular old brown bat that's decided to roost in your attic. Though annoying, these guys eat pesky insects, specifically mosquitoes. Of course, they can poop infected droppings all over your house, and sometimes they have rabies, so it's best to not have them as roommates.

There are only three species of vampire bats, none of which live in Transylvania. They hail from the Americas, from Mexico to Brazil, Chile, and Argentina. I'm more afraid of these bloodsuckers:

LEECHES:
Leeches suck . . . literally. They look like little black blobs that stick to your skin when you go for a swim. They latch on with their mouth-parts and start chugging. It was common practice before modern medicine to use leeches to "clean out" bad blood. In reality, patients were being bled to death. Doctors still sometimes use leeches today, but for good, scientific reason. The leeches can reduce swelling by drinking congested blood out of wounds.

MOSQUITOES:
Not all mosquitoes are suckers. Female mosquitoes use the iron and proteins from animal blood to develop their eggs. They hunt for blood by detecting the carbon dioxide emitted by our sweat. When a mosquito bites into its "prey," it releases some saliva into the bite. The saliva is an anticoagulant, which prevents the blood from clotting and blocking her from getting more blood or choking. The saliva is also the reason we get those itchy little red bumps after being bitten by a mosquito. It carries a protein that can be an irritation to the skin.

COUNT CHOCULA:
Okay, this is kind of a stretch, but a creepy cartoon character *vanting* to eat your cereal is almost as annoying as something drinking your blood. Around Halloween, General Mills releases monster-themed cereal, including Count Chocula, Boo Berry, and Franken Berry. When Franken Berry was first released, it was dyed pink with a harmless food coloring that didn't break down in the body. Ironically, the friendly-looking monster scared a few people when they went to the bathroom and discovered "Frankenberry Stool," aka bright-pink poop!

BELA LUGOSI:
The actor who played Dracula in the film based on the book written by Bram Stoker in 1897. Dracula is easily the most famous vampire, after Edward and the Cullens. If you get a chance to watch the movie, watch Mr. Lugosi's eyes. He doesn't blink once.

VAMPIRE TOOL KIT

Whether you're in Transylvania or Pennsylvania, you never know when you might come across a fanged creature of the night. Here's what's in my vampire kit:

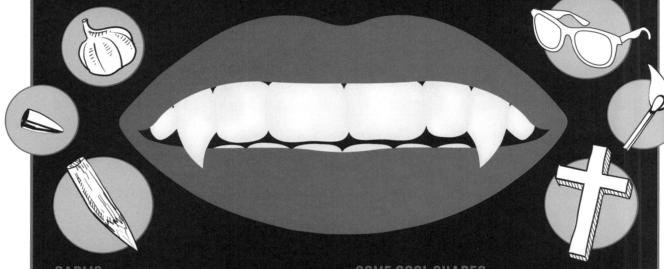

GARLIC: Who knows why vampires don't like garlic? Are they afraid of bad breath?

SILVER: This metal burns the heck out of a vampire. It probably won't kill them, but they'll be in a world of hurt. Kill two birds with one stone with silver bullets just in case you run into a werewolf, too.

WOODEN STAKE: For a creature that is so hard to kill, this tool is pretty simple. The only problem is you have to get close enough to stab it in the heart.

SOME COOL SHADES: If there is one thing vampires can't stand, it's sunlight. So, bring them out into the sun. The sunglasses will protect your eyes while you're destroying a vampire and you'll look pretty hip doing it.

MATCHES: If you can't get a vampire out into the sun, bring its hot, blazing flames to the bloodsucker.

CRUCIFIX: The sign of the cross turns a fiending vamp into a recoiling disaster. Flash it at them and run like heck.

Other Big Bats

HANK AARON: Known as Hammerin' Hank, Hank Aaron hit 755 home runs in his baseball career. Aaron held the record for most career home runs until 2007 when Barry Bonds broke it. Only Aaron, Bonds (1), and Babe Ruth (3) have hit more than 700 career home runs.

ROGER MARIS AND MICKEY MANTLE: In the 1961 season, Maris and Mantle, both New York Yankees, threatened to break Babe Ruth's record for most home runs during one season. As the season went on, the media covered the M&M boys, creating a rivalry between the two that didn't exist in reality. Mantle's ability to "schmooze" with the media gave him the better image. People cheered for Mantle to beat Maris, but in the end, it was Maris who broke the record with sixty-one home runs.

BABE RUTH: You couldn't even discuss the previous three batters without mentioning the Sultan of Swat. The Bambino has been called the greatest batter that has ever lived. He set all of the batting records while he played; most career home runs with 714, most home runs in a single season with 60, most walks, highest slugging percentage, and highest RBI. Not only was he the first to hit sixty home runs in a season, before that he was the first player to hit thirty, forty, and fifty.

WILLIE MAYS: The "Say Hey Kid" has been called the greatest all-around player of all time. He had eight consecutive 100-RBI seasons. In 1955 he hit more than fifty home runs. Ten years later, he did the same thing.

ALBERT PUJOLS: It's tough to stand out among the greats of baseball, but Pujols is holding his ground and he's just started. Pujols currently ranks 45th in the leading home-run hitters in Major League Baseball history and he began playing in the majors in 2001. In 2008, MLB managers voted Pujols the most feared batter in baseball. And with that bat it makes sense they don't like it when he comes up to the plate. Pujols is on pace to become the most prolific hitter of all time, and he's a really nice guy.

grasshoppers

They're high in protein, low in fat, and rich in minerals, not to mention they're delish! After ants, grasshoppers are the most popular insect eaten around the world. Unlike ants, grasshoppers have superior flavor profiles that vary from region to region depending on their diet, and grasshoppers can be cooked any way imaginable. Sautéed in the Philippines and sauced with vinegar, onions, and tomatoes, they make a great stir-fry that takes advantage of that country's grassier-, woodsier-tasting bugs. In Mexico, the nuttier grasshoppers in the Isthmus region are dry roasted and seasoned with lime and salt. Worldwide, grasshoppers can be found on the menu from the Americas to Thailand to Uganda. No matter where you eat them, beware of the grasshopper's legs and wings. They can scratch or get stuck in your throat. And let's not even get into the unsightly look of grasshopper legs in your teeth.

Bizarre Grasshopper Facts

- A large grasshopper packs more than 20 grams of protein, making it a good and plentiful food source. In many countries, military personnel are taught to catch and eat grasshoppers if they have no food.

- Grasshoppers begin their lives as nymphs, which look like tiny white grasshoppers without wings and reproductive organs. After exposure to sunlight, they assume the distinctive colors and markings of adults.

- Ever wonder why these jumping insects are so difficult to catch? Chalk it up to their fantastic eyesight. They have five eyes in total, which allows them to see not only long distances but also forward, backward, and sideways.

- Don't be too ticked if a grasshopper gives you the cold shoulder. They don't have any ears at all.

- If you ever hold a grasshopper, you may notice that it spits a brown liquid on you. This gunk is commonly called "tobacco juice," and may protect them from attacks by predators.

- Not only do a grasshopper's legs allow the insect to go airborne, but they also help with its hygiene. The legs flick away the excess frass (aka insect poop) that's stuck to the grasshopper's body after defecation. The legs are kind of like bug toilet paper.

- Their legs can also make beautiful music. Male grasshoppers can chirp, like crickets, by rubbing their legs against their bodies.

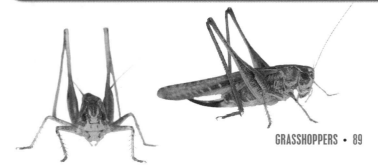

PEST CONTROL

According to the *Guinness World Records,* the desert locust, a type of grasshopper, is the world's most destructive insect. Grasshoppers live anywhere with vegetation and can eat their own weight in food in one day. They love grasses, leaves, and "cereal crops." Swarms of these locusts contain 40 to 80 million grasshoppers at a time, and they can consume 20,000 tons of grain and vegetation in twenty-four hours. With this ability, they can destroy a farm's livelihood in a single day.

CAUTION

Like everything, grasshoppers are best eaten in moderation. Some grasshoppers have been found to contain high levels of lead. And some grasshoppers can contain tapeworms—a parasitic species that latches onto its host's intestine and sucks nutrients from its body. Although grasshoppers can be eaten raw, they are safest to eat after they've been cooked.

CHAPULINES: Grasshoppers, Oaxaca Style

If you find yourself in Oaxaca, Mexico, (pronounced *Wah-hah-kah*) make sure to try the chapulines, the spicy, limey, and garlicky snacking grasshoppers. Mayans, Aztecs, and Zapotecs dined on chapulines more than 3,000 years ago, well before the Spanish arrived in Mexico. Oaxacan legend claims that if you eat chapulines there, you'll always return to the area. Put them on top of tacos for an added crunch or eat them as an on-the-go snack. Walk into any bar in the region and, like peanuts in the United States, bowls of chapulines will be on every countertop.

COOL JUMPING ANIMALS

Grasshoppers are great jumpers. They move quickly by jumping twenty times their own body length. That would be like a human jumping from one end of a basketball court to another in a single bound. If they could figure out how to shoot, these animals would also make an animal dream team:

BHARAL: Also known as a Himalayan blue sheep, these mountain creatures are capable of jumping from rock to rock and hill to hill.

HARE: Hare or jackrabbits move by jumping. Once they get going, they can run up to 45 miles per hour.

RED KANGAROO: The largest species of kangaroo can reach jumping speeds of up to 35 miles per hour.

KLIPSPRINGER: This animal's name translates to "rock jumper" in Afrikaans. They can jump the highest compared to body size among animals. At almost 60 inches tall, they can jump ten times their body height.

KANGAROO RAT: These North American–native rodents are named after their locomotion, which is similar to a kangaroo. These critters jump the farthest compared to body size among mammals, at forty-five times their own body length. This is like a human jumping across a football field, goalpost to goalpost.

FROGHOPPER: The froghopper hops from plant to plant and can jump 28 inches vertically—impressive, considering they're only ¼ inch long at most.

JUMPING SPIDER: This spider can jump 100 times its own body length. This is like a human jumping the length of two jumbo jets.

TREE FROG: This frog can jump 150 times its own length. This is like a human jumping from one end of the *Titanic* to another.

LAST, BUT NOT LEAST, THE MVP . . .

FLEA: Fleas are the best jumpers in the world. They can jump 220 times their own body length and 150 times their body height. If humans could jump 220 times their own body length, they could jump a mile in about five bounds.

Q&A WITH SUSANA TRILLING

Chef Susana Trilling resides in Oaxaca, Mexico, home of some of the best chapulines on the planet. In addition to cooking, writing cookbooks, teaching culinary classes, and hosting television programs, she sometimes hunts for grasshoppers with her kids.

Where do you get your grasshoppers?

If I want to catch and prepare them, I go outside to an alfalfa field nearby and get them, or send my kids. If I want them in a hurry, I buy them in the Etla market on Wednesdays or Sundays. There are women walking around with baskets who sell little bowls full or sometimes the amount is measured in oval sardine cans. I prefer the smaller ones, as with the larger ones, the legs get stuck in my teeth. I have a favorite merchant who sells them and I buy two bags—with and without chili piquin in them. She also sells four kinds of pumpkin seeds at her stand. All things that are crunchy and salty!

When was the first time you tried chapulines? How were they prepared? Who made them?

My friend Maria Taboada made them for me when I first got to Oaxaca. We went out to catch them in the alfalfa fields behind her house with a bag tied on a pole, like a butterfly net. She cooked them in a frying pan with garlic, limes from her trees, and salt. She also fried some whole little chilies called chili piquin that she picked from a bush in her garden, and stirred them in. They were crispy.

How would you describe the taste of grasshoppers?

They taste like salt, garlic, and lime and are crunchy. They can be picante (spicy) or not.

What is your favorite way to eat chapulines?

I love to eat chapulines in a hot, fresh, handmade tortilla with guacamole sauce and sprinkle the chapulines on that and roll it up and eat it!

What goes best with chapulines?

I think the taste of avocado and chapulines combine well and also black beans. (Sometimes I grind them in my beans for flavoring.) They also combine well with maize or dried corn, like in soft tortilla (*blandas*) or larger, crispier tortillas called *tlalludas*. My boyfriend toasts them with pecans. That combines well too.

A MODERATELY FUNNY JOKE

A grasshopper walks into a bar. The bartender says, "Hey, grasshopper! We have a drink named after you." The grasshopper looks at him with a confused look on his face. He says to the bartender, "Why would anyone name a drink Bob?"

For more information on Susana Trilling, check out SeasonsOfMyHeart.com.

Haggis

Just one look at a haggis [HAG-ihs]—cooked innards, organs, and oats spewing from a bloated sheep's stomach—conjures up images of Frankenstein. For my money, this Scottish dish is deservedly the most infamously gory, gritty, and messy. It is also the most seminal. From its humble beginning came *slátur*, haggis's rustic Scandinavian twin; then later, the prettified *boudin noir*, the dish's French great-great-grandchild. In Samoa, tribes sit down to a family meal of whole roast hog, with the most honored guest receiving a special piece of intestine, its curvy, thick tendril stuffed with all the "pluck" (heart, liver, and lungs) and blood, tied and baked, bursting at the seams. Same in Uganda, or on Navajo tribal lands in Monument Valley, Arizona. In Nicaragua, Bolivia, Chile, Belize, and Argentina they serve a stewed version called *chanfaina*, oftentimes adding cornmeal or swollen motes to extend the serving sizes. Every country in the world makes a version of it, but it's all haggis to me.

All the peoples of the world came from traditional hunting-and-gathering tribal groups.

While the skin, fat, muscles, bones, and tendons could be set aside and dealt with at a later time, the pluck and the blood had to be utilized immediately. Remember, these were the days before refrigerators, and while the meat could be smoked, salted, dried, or cooked for later consumption, the naughty bits needed a quick technique for preservation. The ancients solved this puzzle by first taking the heart, lungs, liver, blood, and other offal to the stone grinder, mixing it with grain of some type, adding the blood, and stuffing the whole mess back inside a natural casing (often the stomach or the intestines). Then, they'd plop these bonbons into boiling water or bury them in ash and coal to cook as the rest of the animal was being skinned and parceled out among the hunting brethren. Once cooked, haggis and all its relatives can be dried and preserved for the long winters that followed the autumnal hunting season, and unlike so many of the world's oldest foods (anyone drink mead anymore?), this one has remained popular. Well, sort of.

I am a huge fan of blood sausage and all its kin, but it took a visit to Edinburgh to convince me that haggis, when cooked properly, could be so awesomely delicious. A cold November day in rain-swept Scotland seemed oddly appropriate for my haggis initiation. I ventured out of my hotel and wandered into Crombies, where haggis is still made, fresh each day, by an actual Crombie (third-generation proprietor). Sandy Crombie and I spent an hour over tea disparaging the canned and frozen haggis of the modern world. Can you eat canned stew and say that it's better than the version on Grandma's stove? I think not. Same with haggis.

Next, Sandy led me through the haggis process. We took the heart, lungs, liver, and blood of a lamb, ground it, added Sandy's secret seasoning mix—a well-guarded family secret (I can tell you it's got cumin and coriander in it!)—mixed in some onions, oats, and ground

Haggis in its glory, nestled next to neeps and tatties (turnip mash and potatoes). Delicious!

lamb meat. We stuffed about a hundred of the buggers, and into the massive vertical steamer they went, Sandy pointing out that demand and modern convenience have meant altering the family-recipe cooking instructions a tad. A few hours later we stood salivating over the perfect, plump, moist, ovaloid haggis. Sandy had his massive blade ready, and he drew the edge against the taut stomach lining revealing, for a brief moment, the spreading wound. Then, the guts burst forth in all their glory. We spooned the filling onto the plate nestled next to the neeps and tatties (turnip mash and potatoes). I inhaled the unctuous, rich, and oddly familiar smell. Then it hit me: It reminded me of my grandmother's chopped chicken liver.

Every pub and casual eatery in Scotland serves haggis in some form. The renaissance of reworked and re-imagined traditional foods has helped drive many young chefs to the recipe books of their ancestors, but the popularity has as much to do with the taste as with the cult of food worship that currently exists in Europe, Asia, and the Americas. Haggis is good stuff. Its deep, mineral, earthy flavor is truly unique, especially when cooked fresh. Anyone who eats French pâté, or bologna, hot dogs, hash, or salami shouldn't raise their nose to the humble haggis, which declares, "I am what I am," in louder and more truthful tones than any of those dangerously disguised foods.

Address to a Haggis
by Robert Burns
(translated by Andrew Zimmern)

Fair fa' your honest, sonsie face,
Great chieftain o' the pudding race!
Aboon them a' ye tak your place,
Painch, tripe, or thairm:
Weel are ye wordy o' a grace
As lang's my arm.

The groaning trencher there ye fill,
Your hurdies like a distant hill,
Your pin wad help to mend a mill
In time o' need,
While thro' your pores the dews distil
Like amber bead.

His knife see rustic Labour dight,
An' cut you up wi' ready sleight,
Trenching your gushing entrails bright,
Like ony ditch;
And then, O what a glorious sight,
Warm-reeking, rich!

Then, horn for horn,
they stretch an' strive:
Deil tak the hindmost! on they drive,
Till a' their weel-swall'd kytes belyve,
Are bent lyke drums;
Then auld Guidman, maist like to rive,
Bethankit! hums.

Dang, haggis!
Your deliciousness is beyond compare—
stomach, guts & innards
all cooked together? Yum!
You FREAKING ROCK!

Did you know "hurdies"
means "buttocks"?

And that part about the "pores distilling"
refers to the juices
oozing out of the haggis'
casing (aka a sheep's stomach!)

When you cut the haggis open,
guts & grains & stuff gush
out like crazy —
and they're piping hot, too!

The people Burns is talking
about keep stuffing their
face with the stuff inside
the haggis until
their bellies are full
and everyone has to
"rive" aka "belch".
Awesome!

ODE TO HAGGIS

Robert Burns solidified the importance of haggis in Scottish culture with his homage to the dish in "Address to a Haggis." Burns considered haggis a symbolic part of Scottish identity and used the humble food as a vehicle to demonstrate his Scottish nationalism. Additionally, he wanted to give all Scots the thumbs-up to belch after eating said haggis.

The Wild Haggis: Fact or Fiction?

According to Scottish folklore, wild haggis exist in the Scottish Highlands (though photos of the animal are rare). We hear a haggis is a small four-legged creature, with limbs shorter on one side, and can easily be caught by running around the hill in the opposite direction. Hmm . . . something about that story sure seems fishy, but that doesn't keep the Scots from leading tourists on hunting expeditions.

AN AWARD-WINNING HAGGIS

Canadian screenwriter, producer, and director Paul Haggis wrote *Million Dollar Baby* and *Crash*, becoming the first individual to have written Best Picture Oscar winners in two consecutive years.

A STOMACH FULL OF STOMACH

On October 8, 2008, competitive eater Eric "Steakbellie" Livingston set a world record by consuming 3 pounds of haggis in eight minutes.

HEY—IT'S SAFER THAN FLAMING PINS

A haggis juggling contest that takes place at the Scottish Juggling Convention each year, with entrants competing for how long they can juggle three, four, or five large haggis.

I THINK I'M GONNA HURL

Haggis is used in a sport called haggis hurling, which involves throwing a haggis as far as possible. The present Guinness World Record has been held by Alan Pettigrew for more than twenty-five years. He threw a 1.5-pound haggis 180 feet, 10 inches on the island of Inchmurrin, Loch Lomond, in August 1984.

CROMBIES' HAGGIS-MAKIN' METHOD

It's said that only dying has a worse reputation than haggis, but that hasn't stopped the Crombie family from hawking the stuff for three generations. Here's how they make this bizarre food in their Edinburgh butcher shop.

STEP 1: Boil the pluck (lamb hearts, lungs, and liver).

STEP 2: Mix suet, onions, and lamb breast with the cooked pluck. Run through industrial grinder, creating a delicious organ-meat confetti.

STEP 3: Add oatmeal and the Crombies' secret seasoning (you'll just have to improvise—try salt, pepper, sugar, thyme, cumin, coriander, fresh parsley, and garlic).

STEP 4: Squeeze ground meat into tube of sheep intestine (you have one in your fridge, right?), filling loosely so the thing doesn't explode in the oven.

STEP 5: Once cooked, slice that haggis open and eat. It's traditionally served with tatties and neeps with a savory whisky sauce.

MAKE YOUR OWN KILT

Kilts and haggis are the pinnacle of Scottish tradition. Some folks claim the kilt originated with the men of the Scottish Highlands in the sixteenth century, but others say it's much older than that. Certainly part of its allure stems from convenience: Whether you're a shepherd or a soldier, it's easier to relieve yourself in a skirt. (This is also why the traditional kilt-wearing opt to "go commando.") And yes, you must still wash your hands afterward.

Here's how to create a kilt of your own: Take 4 to 6 yards of tartan fabric, depending on your gut size. Measure distance from knees to the waist, then around the waist and hips. Kilt should hit at the kneecap, leaving half an inch for the hem. Cut fabric to measure.

Wrap tartan around the waist. Make inch-wide pleats along the back of the kilt, pinning them in place. Make sure the measurements for all the pleats are equal.

Remove the kilt with the pins intact from the dummy. Sew the tops of the pleats down.

Create waistband with spare fabric. It should be roughly 4 inches wide, and long enough to wrap around the waist. Fold in half and sew to the top of the kilt. Cut two 10-inch-long, inch-wide strips of Velcro. Sew onto the waistband where ends of the kilt will meet.

Press the pleats with a hot iron. Place a slightly damp piece of cotton between the iron and the pleats to keep the pleats permanently in place. Ta-da!

Headcheese

Headcheese is a meat jelly made from the head of a calf, pig, or sheep, typically served in aspic. "Aspic" may sound like a poisonous chemical, but it's in fact just chopped-up ingredients held together with meat stock or consommé infused with gelatin. Meat jellies became popular many centuries ago when the head of an animal was cleaned (oftentimes the eyes, ears, and brain were already removed) and simmered to produce stock. When the stock cools, it becomes gummy, and firm from by-products derived from the skull's natural gelatin and collagen. The unpleasant parts of the head (bones, eyelashes, etc.) could be discarded, and the meat could be pulled from all the nooks and crannies. Cooks found that after discarding the inedible parts the meat could be packed into pots or molds, and the cooled liquid could be poured over the meat, cooled further until set, and then served. It's a great way to preserve meat. The jelly keeps air and bacteria out, while sealing flavor in. And it's delicious!

There are as many recipes around the world for headcheese made from all different types of animals as there are cooks looking to make it. The most unusual headcheese I have ever eaten is one made from a moose head that when finished included the lips and nose, thus very deserving of the name moose nose jelly. It was a little gamey but quite tasty, especially with strong mustard and a good rye bread.

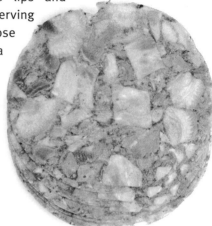

Breaking down a pig's head the old-fashioned way at Lindy & Grundy in Los Angeles.

Get Jiggly With It!

Your favorite jiggling dessert just got freaky! Did you know gelatin is a protein produced from collagen? About a third of the human body is made of collagen—a big, fibrous molecule that makes skin, bones, and tendons both strong and somewhat elastic. The gelatin you eat in JELL-O comes from the collagen in cow or pig bones, hooves, and connective tissues.

To make gelatin, these animal parts are ground up and treated with either a strong acid or a strong base to release the collagen. The resulting mixture is boiled and eventually becomes gelatin. The gelatin is easily extracted because it forms a wobbly layer on the surface of the boiling mixture.

It's hard to say who came up with the idea to grind bones and hooves, cook them down, add sugar and artificial flavoring, cool the mixture, and then eat it. However, Peter Cooper, an industrialist and builder of the first American steam-powered locomotive, obtained the patent for powdered gelatin in 1845. Mr. Cooper, I salute you.

CHEESE HEADS

Don't get headcheese confused with cheese heads. While neither are really cheese, cheese heads are not edible. A cheese head is the name for someone from Wisconsin, and now it more specifically refers to fans of the NFL's Green Bay Packers. The name started as a derogatory term from Illinois football and baseball fans to make fun of their opposing Wisconsin teams. Wisconsin fans took the name on proudly, claiming the title. In 1987, Ralph Bruno, a fan, made himself a hat out of foam that looked like Swiss cheese. He wore the hat to a Milwaukee Brewers game and started to sell them after the hats gained attention. Today, Lambeau Field is filled with the yellow foam hats.

FAMOUS CHEESE HEADS

Magician **HARRY HOUDINI** (1874–1926) was actually born in Budapest, Hungary, though he claimed Appleton, Wisconsin—the town he immigrated to—as his place of birth.

Known as the King of Bling, **WLADZIU VALENTINO LIBERACE** (1919–1987) took up the piano at the age of four in West Allis, Wisconsin.

You can thank artist and Racine, Wisconsin, native **JOYCE CARLSON** (1923–2008) for some of your favorite Disney theme-park rides, including It's a Small World. Good luck getting that song

out of your head for the rest of the day!

Though she fell in love with the American Southwest later in life, artist **GEORGIA O'KEEFFE** (1887–1986) hailed from Sun Prairie, Wisconsin.

Regarded as the greatest film of all time, *Citizen Kane* was directed by and starred Kenosha native **ORSON WELLES** (1915–1985).

One of America's most famous and influential architects, **FRANK LLOYD WRIGHT** (1867–1959), was born

in the quaint farming town of Richland Center, Wisconsin.

Before he was Willy Wonka, **GENE WILDER** (1933–) attended Milwaukee's Washington High School with fellow classmates **BUD SELIG** (commissioner of Major League Baseball) and U.S. Senator **HERB KOHL**.

Milwaukee-born actor **SPENCER TRACY** (1900–1967) won two Academy Awards, and earned a top-ten spot in the American Film Institute's list of Greatest Male Stars of All Time.

Speaking of Gelatin . . .

Marshmallow is a plant native to Africa, scientifically named *Althaea officinalis*. Ancient Egyptians made the first marshmallows from the root of the plant. Their original purpose was to soothe a sore throat. Marshmallows were hard to make. In the nineteenth century, French manufacturers developed a marshmallow recipe, using gelatin with a combination of sugar, corn syrup, dextrose, and water, whipped into a spongy consistency. These are the marshmallows we know today. The following are the best uses for the fluffy treats:

HOT COCOA:
Add them to your hot cocoa during the winter to give your drink a little extra flavor.

S'MORES:
They made their first appearance in the *Girl Scout Handbook* in 1927, and now s'mores make regular appearances around the campfire. The combination of graham crackers, chocolate, and marshmallows will have you always wanting "some more."

FLUFFERNUTTER SANDWICH:
Popular in the northeastern United States, the Fluffernutter sandwich is simply peanut butter and Marshmallow Fluff between two slices of bread.

RICE KRISPIES TREATS:
The combination of a rice cereal and marshmallows that is both crisp and gooey—a delicious combo.

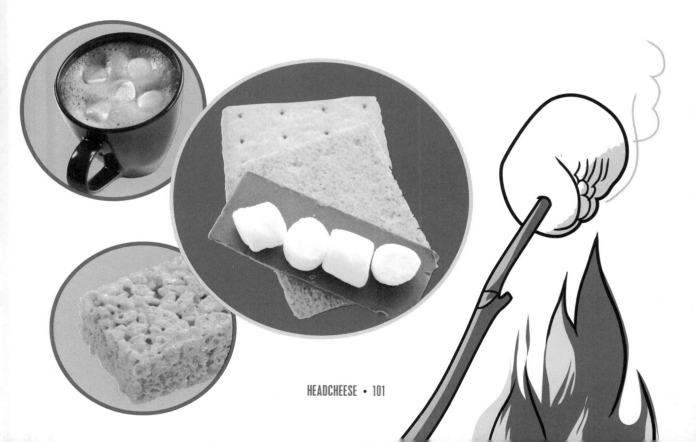

MARIO BATALI: The Head Cheese

Known for his larger-than-life personality, orange Crocs, and bold approach to food, Mario Batali is more than a chef—he's a rock star. He also makes some of the best headcheese I've ever tasted. The man himself explains his lifelong love affair with this offally delicious treat.

When did you try headcheese for the first time? Who made it?

I was fifteen on a trip with my dad and my brother in 1975, and it was in a little country restaurant outside of Pau in France. It was house made and was my appetizer with sauce gribiche. My main course that day was calves' brains with *beurre noir* and capers.

Where does your headcheese recipe come from?

We create it ourselves at [my restaurants] Otto, Del Posto, and Babbo in New York City and at B&B in Las Vegas, and each one is a little different.

How do you make headcheese?

Brine the head, then roast it with spices, then shred the meat by hand, roughly chopping the big pieces, and then lay them in a round tureen and chill.

What's the key to making a successful head-cheese?

A good head. Fine, well-sourced pork is the whole game.

Why do you think headcheese "disappeared" from American menus? Why did you decide to put headcheese on the menu at Babbo?

I think as America became richer, we felt less of the need for the artistry of whole-animal cookery. I put it on the menu at Babbo in 1998 to express my passion for traditional Italian cooking and to celebrate the whole animal's use. We also have brains, liver, kidneys, ears, and feet on the menu almost all of the time.

Why is headcheese suddenly all the rage in the culinary world?

I think responsible animal use is making a lot of sense to thoughtful cooks, and besides that, it is simply delicious.

Best way to serve headcheese?

I like the slices placed on a warm plate with a few pickled onions.

What is the most bizarre thing you've ever eaten?

Casu marzu (see page 126).

Hot Dogs

At least several times a year the following passion play ensues.

THE SCENE: I am with my son sitting in our seats at the Twins game at Target Field in Minneapolis.

FAN (*walks up or down steps, eating a hot dog as he goes, notices us, and stops*): Hey, you're Andrew Zimmern. How do you stomach eating some of that stuff I see you chowing down on every week on *Bizarre Foods*? That stuff in Africa was so gross, what was that? Grilled porcupine? Or that meat in Thailand, was that a rodent? Ugh.

ME: Well, sir, that's kind of ironic. The hot dog you are eating is made of chlorinated ammonia–rinsed animal parts of unknown origin, bought at auction, shipped out of country in many cases, liquidized and cleansed, and shipped back here. It's made into sausages and contains parts of animals that many of us feel are unsafe to eat on any terms. Need further proof that commercially prepared dogs are strange? Our government has laws that prevent you and me from even checking out the facilities they are made in or knowing what's in them!

What's the old adage, "no one wants to see how laws or hot dogs are made"? Well, I want to see that! And I think you should also. At least when I eat porcupine in Botswana and rice field rats in Thailand I know that the meat is fresh and unadulterated and where it comes from. I would ask you, sir, to be more open-minded. The hot

Mmmm! Lips, buttholes, and animal trimmings sound delicious when you call them a hot dog.

dog you hold in your hand is all fat, lips, and buttholes. Enjoy!

The end.

MOMMY, WHERE DO HOT DOGS COME FROM?

Hot dogs are typically made from meat trim that has been left over after a butcher processes his animals into more saleable cuts. This includes bits of organs and bone, which means some of these tube steaks pack a nice punch of calcium. Traditionally, the casing that the hot dogs are made in is from animal intestines. When you think about it, commercially made American hot dogs are one of the most bizarre foods on the planet, and one of the most disgusting on hundreds of levels. What's even weirder is that Americans consume about 7 billion hot dogs between Memorial Day and Labor Day every year.

Bizarre Hot Dog Facts

- Hot dogs were first sold at a baseball game in St. Louis, Missouri, in 1893.

- Ever wonder why it's called a wiener? It's named after the city in which it was invented. While Americans know the place as Vienna, Austria, it's actually called Wien in German.

- The first Coney Island hot-dog stand was opened in 1871 by Charles Feltman. He sold 3,684 "dachshund sausages in milk rolls" in the first year.

- In 1957, the U.S. Chamber of Commerce named July Hot Dog Month.

- Twenty-six million hot dogs are consumed at baseball parks in one year.

- Sara Lee Corporation created the world's longest hot dog in 1996. The wiener, made in honor of that year's Olympic Games in Atlanta, measured 1,996 feet. Though the actual meat of the dog was continuous, the bun was not.

- On average, every person in the United States eats sixty hot dogs per year. New Yorkers eat the most hot dogs.

- The most popular hot-dog topping is mustard for adults and ketchup for children.

- The average hot dog is eaten in 6.1 bites.

- It is recommended that hot dogs be grilled using tongs or a spatula, because forks can pierce the hot dog and release tasty juices.

History of the Hot Dog

Sausage has been around for thousands of years, but the wiener has only been around for a few hundred years. What we now call a hot dog was supposedly created in the late 1600s by a German butcher named Johann Georghehner. This red sausage reminded people of a dachshund (aka wiener dog) and was served hot, thus the name hot dog.

The Chicago Dog

Few people relish the hot dog as much as Chicagoans do. The Windy City boasts more hot-dog joints than McDonald's, Wendy's, and Burger King—combined! And though you can get a hot dog topped with anything from just mustard to foie gras, the classic Chicago dog is served on a poppy-seed bun and topped with yellow mustard, chopped white onions, sweet neon-green pickle relish, a dill pickle spear, tomato slices, pickled peppers, and a dash of celery salt. A true Chicago dog never includes ketchup. Ever.

The Wienermobile

The Wienermobile was created in 1936 by Carl G. Mayer, nephew of Oscar Mayer, to promote Oscar Mayer wieners. Because gas was rationed during World War II, the Wienermobile didn't hit the streets until the 1950s. The car was made from a Dodge Chassis or a Willys Jeep Chassis. Here are the vanity plates the Wienermobile has had:

YUMMY

OUR DOG

IWSHIWR

OH I WISH

WEENR

WNRMOBL

BOLOGNA

RELSHME

LIL LINK

BIG BUN

WNR MBLE

Competitive Eating

Competitive eating is most popular in the United States, but there is an International Federation of Competitive Eating. The IFOCE is responsible for official Major League Eating competitions and hands out more than $230,000 in prize money each year.

One of the federation's most "prestigious" competitions is Nathan's Famous Hot Dog Eating Contest. The annual contest is held at New York's Coney Island every July 4 and draws throngs of gurgitators (aka sport eaters) and spectators alike.

In 2009, Joey "Jaws" Chestnut of San Jose, California, downed sixty-eight hot dogs and buns in ten minutes, and holds the record for most hot dogs consumed at the Nathan's Famous Hot Dog Eating Contest.

RECORDS FOR OTHER FOODS IN THE BOOK

LOBSTER ROLLS

DATE: September 23, 2006
PLACE: Boston, MA
AMOUNT: 41 lobster rolls
TIME: 10 minutes
WINNER: Takeru Kobayashi

HAGGIS

DATE: October 8, 2008
PLACE: Philadelphia, PA
AMOUNT: 3 pounds
TIME: 8 minutes
WINNER: Eric Livingston

ROCKY MOUNTAIN OYSTERS

DATE: August 8, 2010
PLACE: Isle Black Hawk Rocky Mountain Oyster Eating World Championship, Black Hawk, CO
AMOUNT: 3 lbs, 11.75 ounces
TIME: 10 minutes
WINNER: Pat Bertoletti

SPAM

DATE: April 3, 2004
PLACE: Spamarama; Austin, TX
AMOUNT: 6 pounds of SPAM from the can
TIME: 12 minutes
WINNER: Richard LeFevre

TURDUCKEN

DATE: November 26, 2003
PLACE: Thanksgiving Meal Invitational, New York, NY
AMOUNT: 7.75 pounds of Thanksgiving meal, including turducken, green beans, cranberry sauce, and yams
TIME: 12 minutes
WINNER: Sonya Thomas

SPAM—the meat product, not the junk email!

Famous Hot Dogs

HOT-DOG \'hät-'dȯg\ verb: to perform in a conspicuous or often ostentatious manner; especially to perform fancy stunts and maneuvers; to show off

ARTHUR HERBERT FONZARELLI

Known by most as Fonzie, this guy might be the biggest hot dog to grace the small screen. The *Happy Days* character, with slicked-back hair, jeans, leather jacket, and motorcycle, is the epitome of cool. The Fonz did his fair share of hot-dogging; he's best known for successfully jumping a shark while on water skis during the fifth season of *Happy Days*.

PHILIPPE PETIT

On August 7, 1974, twenty-four-year-old Petit stepped out on a ¾-inch-thick wire illegally rigged between the World Trade Center towers. After spending nearly an hour dancing on the high wire hoisted 1,350 feet above New York City, Petit simply walked back to one of the towers, where he was then arrested. Public appreciation for Petit's act convinced police to drop all official charges for what is dubbed the "artistic crime of the century." A film which chronicled Petit's infamous walk, *Man on Wire*, won the Oscar for Best Documentary in 2009.

EVEL KNIEVEL

The original American daredevil, Evel Knievel rose to fame in the sixties and seventies with a series of ramp-to-ramp motorcycle jumps. Though Knievel experienced many epic failures (*Guinness World Records* recognizes him as the survivor of "most bones broken in a lifetime"—433 in his 69 years), his stunts were some of the most watched in history.

JOHNNY KNOXVILLE

One of the masterminds behind the hugely successful *Jackass* series, Knoxville made his mark via self-inflicted wounds. Sure, taking a bullet to the chest (while wearing a bulletproof vest . . . but still), allowing a

Hot-dogging at the skate park. Where's your helmet, kid?

baby gator to clamp onto his exposed nipple, and unleashing a mist of Mace to the face aren't really "smart ideas," and yet it seems both Knoxville and the rest of us can't get enough.

DONALD TRUMP

A show-off of a completely different nature, the Trumpster can't seem to stop himself from broadcasting his fame and fortune to the world. Trump International golf courses, Trump International Hotels, Trump-run beauty pageants (Miss Universe), Trump television shows, even Trump brand bottled water.

Hot-dogging at a press conference: Donald Trump.

JUICY LUCY

The Juicy Lucy is a cheeseburger. Plain and simple.

But for millions of obsessive burger freaks in the Midwest this is where the comparison ends. A Juicy Lucy (also known as a Jucy Lucy) has cheese in the center of the patty rather than on top.

The cheese is built inside of two thin raw patties before being grilled or griddled, and it melts while the burger cooks, resulting in a molten cheese that tends to gush out at the first bite.

(WARNING: It is advised to be careful and wait for the burger to cool a little, so as to not burn one's mouth. That cheese is HOT! Trust me when I say that there are more burn-related oral injuries as a result of premature Juicy Lucy eating per capita than the often heralded but overly dramatized pizza-mouth burns we all hear so much about.)

The inside-out cheeseburger hails from Minneapolis. However, its exact place of birth is still under question. Matt's Bar and the 5-8 Club, both on Cedar Avenue in Minneapolis, claim to have invented this grilled staple. The bars use different spellings for the burgers: Matt's calls the burger a "Jucy Lucy," while 5-8 Club spells it "Juicy Lucy." Servers at the 5-8 wear T-shirts reading, "If it's spelled right, it's done right." Matt's Bar retaliated with shirts that read, "If it's spelled correctly, you're at the wrong place." So who does the best Lucy? Try both and decide for yourself.

DIY JUICY LUCY

- Squish ⅔ pound of ground beef (the fattier, the better) into two patties.

- Grab a slice of cheese (American is the traditional choice, but feel free to go crazy with other kinds—Swiss, pepperjack, Limburger . . . whatever you like), break into quarters, and place in the center of one of the patties.

- Take the other patty and lay it on the cheese-topped one. Fuse the two patties together by pinching around the edges, making sure there's no place for the cheese to escape.

- Grill the burger for about eight minutes with the lid closed. Flip the burger, poke a hole in the top for steam to escape (you don't want a cheesy volcanic eruption on your hands!), and grill for about six more minutes.

- Hard part: Let burger sit for at least three minutes so you don't burn the bejesus out of your mouth! There's molten hot cheese in there!

- I like to top mine with the classics—ketchup, yellow mustard, and pickles on a soft white bun.

HOW to Treat a Mouth Burn

So. You didn't wait before biting into that Juicy Lucy, did you? Amateur! Quick, follow these steps:

1. Put an ice cube in your mouth to minimize pain and swelling.

2. Eat something cold like a Popsicle or ice cream.

3. Avoid eating hot foods, or foods that are spicy, salty, or citrus.

LOVABLE LUCYS

Who couldn't love the first lady of comedy, **LUCILLE BALL**? She's the fiery redhead whose never-ending quest for success and stardom always resulted in hilarious predicaments.

Don't mess with **LUCY LAWLESS**—star of the internationally successful cult classic television series *Xena: Warrior Princess*. She can wield a sword and kick butt in a tiny skirt (without messing up her flowing locks).

LUCILLE VAN PELT (above, far right), known by *Peanuts* fans as Lucy, is crabby and cynical, especially for an eight-year-old. She is also well known for running a psychiatric booth, a parody of lemonade stands.

Unearthed in 1974, this Lucy might be the world's most famous early human ancestor. The 3.2-million-year-old ape **LUCY** was the first *Australopithecus afarensis* skeleton ever found. Discovered in Ethiopia, her remains are only about 40 percent complete.

One of the original stars of the silver screen, **LUCILLE FAY LeSUEUR** (better known as Joan Crawford), had a temper that was almost as well known as her mug. Check out those dramatic eyebrows!

KOPI LUWAK

For those who seek a killer caffeine buzz, kopi luwak may be the Holy Grail. This Indonesian coffee is one of the rarest and most expensive beverages in the world. A pound of primo beans garners upwards of $500, and a single, thimble-sized cup of the brew can go for ten bucks a pop. So what makes this coffee so special? This tasty beverage comes from coffee beans that have been passed through and pooped out of the common palm civet's digestive tract. This cat-sized mammal, which sports the facial markings of a raccoon and is a relative of the mongoose, dines on ripe coffee berries falling from Indonesia's treetops. The fruit is fully digested by the luwak, but the bean remains intact. Farmers then pluck the beans from the fecal matter. After a thorough scrubbing, they're roasted, ground, and brewed.

It's curious why people would shell out so much cash for coffee culled from the dung of a cat-sized, raccoon-like mammal, but it's even more puzzling when you consider who decided

to try this brewing technique in the first place. Like many odd foods, kopi luwak was born out of necessity. In the eighteenth century, Holland established the Dutch East Indies—a nationalized colony in Java and Sumatra. Between 1830 and 1870, the Dutch government instated a policy that required a portion of agricultural production to be designated as an export. The Dutch prohibited native farmers to pick coffee for their own use. Natives still wanted coffee and discovered that the luwak dumped the treasured beans in their droppings, providing Indonesians with the means to brew a surprisingly low in acid, silky smooth, full-bodied, and sweet cup of joe.

Downing a coffee once bound by turd is perfectly safe to drink after the washing, roasting, and brewing process. As for the coffee's flavor, it's absolutely delicious. Then again, so is much of Indonesia's coffee. If you're looking for a fun novelty item, grab a cup of kopi luwak, but if you're just looking for your daily caffeine fix, stick to something that costs less than a car payment.

OTHER THINGS FOUND IN POOP:
DUNG BEETLES
FOOTPRINTS
CORN

Other "Recycled" Foods

JACU BIRD COFFEE: Brazilians dig this beverage derived from the jacu bird's droppings. The birds consume ripe coffee berries, and much like the palm civet, poop out the beans whole.

WEASEL COFFEE: Some Vietnamese weasels eat coffee berries and regurgitate them in the forest. The berries are collected and made into a lovely coffee drink.

HONEY: Your favorite sweetener just got funky. Bees collect nectar from flowers and store it in their "honey stomachs." The insects secrete enzymes that convert the nectar into a sweet, sticky substance, which when upchucked we call honey and spread liberally on a piece of buttered toast.

ARGAN NUT OIL: Goats in Tiout, Morocco, dine on fruit from the tops of the argan tree. Once the fruit is consumed, the goats either spit or poop out the fruit's pit. The kernels are then ground and pressed to make a nutty oil used in cooking or as an antiaging skin-care product.

BIRD'S NEST SOUP: See page 7.

Coffee Facts

- Ethiopian shepherds noticed the effects of coffee when they realized their goats became jumpy after eating coffee berries.

- In 1675, the king of England banned coffeehouses, because he thought people would conspire against him there.

- Coffee grows on trees, which can reach a height of about 30 feet tall.

- After oil, coffee is the most widely traded commodity in the world.

- "Cup of joe" comes from World War II because American soldiers (called GI Joes) were big coffee drinkers. The term "Americano" refers to the way American soldiers would order their espresso during the war: diluted with water.

COMMON COFFEE DRINKS

ESPRESSO: An espresso shot is made by forcing pressurized, hot water through very finely ground coffee beans. Note that it's spelled ESpresso, not EXpresso. EXpresso is a workspace for Microsoft Office communities, as well as an airline in the African country of Mozambique.

AMERICANO: A shot of espresso diluted with enough water to fill a mug.

LATTE: Two espresso shots, topped with steamed milk to fill, and finished with frothy milk.

MOCHA: A latte, with a boost of chocolate.

If you're a coffee freak like me, Seattle is the promised land.

DECAF: Coffee for people who actually like to sleep at night.

INSTANT COFFEE: Coffee for people who are too lazy to brew their own, or don't like their coffee to taste very good. Instant coffee companies will try to tell you otherwise, but it's all rubbish.

COLD PRESS: Ground coffee soaked in water for hours, filtered, and served on ice.

FRAPPUCCINO: More candy than coffee, especially if you order it with lots of extras: Venti soy mocha Frappuccino with whipped cream, mocha drizzle, and coconut flakes. Put on your big-boy pants and get an espresso.

DOES COFFEE STUNT YOUR GROWTH?

You may have heard that coffee will stunt your growth. That threat is about as real as the chances of you crossing your eyes and having them stay that way permanently. Though a cup of joe won't make you a shorty pants, drinking too much of it (especially if you drink soda or eat lots of caffeinated foods, like chocolate) might keep you up all night. It's best to consume your caffeine in moderation.

Liver

A variety of animals gloriously lend their livers to the food world. Beef, chicken, duck, and goose livers, also known colloquially and collectively as foie gras, monkfish liver, and pig liver, are just a few of these organs that end up on the global table. Liver can be baked, broiled, grilled, sautéed, and boiled. It can be stir-fried, fried, or eaten raw. And it can be made into wursts and terrines, sausages and forcemeats, which are a mixture of ground, lean meat emulsified with fat. Yum!

Liver is rich in iron and vitamin A. In fact, liver has so much vitamin A that if someone eats too much of it, it can become poisonous. Liver is most often sold at grocery stores pre-sliced, but if you have the option, go for the whole liver. When the liver is sliced, it "bleeds," letting its moisture seep out. Liver flavor and texture all depend on the ages of the animal, the size of the liver, how fresh the liver is, and how the liver was prepared. If you get the right combination of all four, the meal is exquisite; if

the meat is out of whack, the offal might taste awful.

And a word to the wise: You might want to cross polar bear liver off of your shopping list. C'mon, it's on there, isn't it? Many an Arctic explorer has fallen gravely ill after consuming it. The problem with polar bear liver, as well as other Arctic animals like seals and huskies, is that it contains extremely high levels of retinol, a form of vitamin A. While some vitamins dissolve in water, vitamin A only dissolves in fat. Instead of exiting the body through urine, it collects in the body's filtration organ, the liver. Overconsumption of vitamin A results in a chronic condition called hypervitaminosis A. Symptoms include drowsiness, irritability, severe headache, bone pain, blurred vision, and nausea. In some cases, sufferers reported peeling skin—anything from light flaking around the mouth to full-body skin loss. In extreme cases, some experienced a total shedding of the skin on the pads of their feet, leaving them bloody and exposed. The worst cases ended in severe liver damage, coma, and death.

YOUR LIVER

The liver is a vital organ, meaning its function is necessary to sustain your life. It has many jobs in the human body, including detoxification and the production of both hormones and bile (the stuff that helps digest fats and makes poop brown). The liver is the only organ in the human body that can regenerate, or regrow, itself. At least 25 percent of a healthy liver must be present to regenerate. This is helpful for people who need new livers. Donors can give 25 percent of their liver to a recipient. In successful cases, both parties will regenerate a healthy, functioning liver.

In Greek mythology, Prometheus broke a promise to one of the gods by gifting fire to humankind. He was brutally punished, chained to a rock, where a vulture would peck out his liver every day. His liver regenerated every night, allowing the torture to continue indefinitely. Nice.

JOHN "LIVER-EATING" JOHNSTON

John Garrison was born in Little York, New Jersey, around 1824. During the Civil War, Garrison joined the Confederate Army. One day, he got angry with one of his commanding officers and assaulted him. Garrison changed his name to John Johnston and deserted the army.

It is said that he married a Native American woman and lived a happy life until one day in 1847 when a group of Crow Indians killed her. He started a twelve-year war against the tribe. Every time he killed a man, he would cut out their liver and eat it. This was a great insult to the tribe because the Crow Indians believed the liver housed the soul. They believed if you ate the liver of an animal, you gained its vitality.

This fabulous tale is exactly that—an exaggerated tall tale from the days of the Wild West. Though it appears Johnston enjoyed a good liver, it was probably in the form of beef. He's also said to have been a bootlegger, a mountain man, a soldier lost at sea, a star in a touring Wild West show (with none other than Calamity Jane), and a friend—not foe—to the Crow. Who knows exactly what this legendary man of the wild frontier was really about, but one thing is certain—he was probably the kind of guy you didn't want to double-cross.

FOIE GRAS

Translating to "fat liver" in French, foie gras is a goose or duck liver that has been fattened by force-feeding grain, typically corn, to the bird. This process, called gavage, dates back to 2500 BC in ancient Egypt. Birds were force-fed to fatten them up before butchering.

Egyptians discovered that wild Nile River fowl gorge themselves in preparation for migrations. Migratory birds naturally store fat in their livers to prepare for long flights, where they torch calories and don't eat much food. As the birds chow like crazy, the fat cells in the liver multiply and enlarge the liver. Thus, the Egyptians took to force-feeding the birds in captivity in order to achieve the same result.

Much later, travelers brought the foie gras recipe to France, where it became a sought-after and prized delicacy. Today, France is its biggest producer, but it is popular throughout Europe and the United States. Foie gras ranges from light gray to rose pink, depending on how it's cooked. The best foie gras is solid in color and free of blemishes, with a silken smooth texture and a buttery, mineral taste with an aroma of nutty grain, often due to the bird's diet.

What foie gras looks like at a fancy restaurant.

What it looks like fresh off the farm.

THE LIFE OF A FOIE GRAS BIRD

After the baby bird hatches, it roams around the farm, eating grass. This toughens and strengthens its esophagus, so it's ready for force-feeding later in its life.

As the bird becomes an adolescent, it's given an all-you-can-eat grain mash diet for four weeks. At this point the liver is about half of its goal weight.

Next, when the bird reaches adulthood it's placed in tight quarters with other birds, so all they can do is eat and sleep. The restriction of movement makes it impossible for the birds to exercise off any weight.

For the last two weeks of the bird's life, it's fed two or three times per day through a flexible pipe. The pipe is filled with boiled corn mixed with fat. At this point, the foie gras bird's liver weighs about 400 to 900 grams. The average liver of a duck or a goose weighs about 76 grams.

The plump birds are then brought to the slaughterhouse within fifteen days of force-feeding because they typically die soon after. If the force-feeding is stopped, the birds will return to their normal state.

CONTROVERSY

The production of foie gras is quite controversial. Many people feel the process of force-feeding the birds is inhumane. In some places, like Italy, Germany, Argentina, and parts of the United States, it is illegal. In France, the law protects foie gras production, stating, "Foie gras belongs to the protected cultural and gastronomical heritage of France." Foie gras is also controversial among chefs. Some, like Wolfgang Puck and Albert Roux, have spoken out against serving the dish. Others, like Anthony Bourdain and Michael Ruhlman, argue that as long as the chefs are ordering their foie gras from a farm that produces their birds humanely, it's a fine thing to serve. I agree. I think the stuff is delicious and you can have my terrine of foie gras when you pry it from my cold dead fingers.

YOU SAY FLOCK, I SAY GAGGLE

Collective nouns for various groups of animals, birds, or insects range from obvious (flock of ducks) to ridiculous (a gaggle of geese). Some of my favorites:

A mob of cattle • A bloat of hippopotami • A murder of crows • A troop of monkeys • A parliament of owls • A pandemonium of parrots • A prickle of porcupines • A rhumba of rattlesnakes • A fever of stingrays • A ballet of swans • A creep of tortoises • A mute of hares • A kindergarten of giraffes • A business of ferrets • A pounce of cats • A tribe of baboons

DUCK, DUCK . . . ?

We all played some version of this game as kindergartners. Everyone sits in a circle while one kid taps you on the head. Duck . . . duck . . . then what? This game is played across the United States. Most people would yell "goose!" inciting the last tapped head to get up and chase the picker around the circle. In Minnesota, the picker yells "gray duck!" I don't get it.

OTHER VARIATIONS OF THE GAME

EXTREME DUCK, DUCK, GOOSE: Same picking rules, but once the "goose" is chosen, he or she takes off in the opposite direction of the picker. Wrestling is encouraged.

PATO, PATO, GONSO: The exact same as duck, duck, goose—only in Spanish.

DRIP, DRIP, SPLASH: Instead of tapping people, the picker drips a cup of water on their heads. When the picker dumps the entire cup of water over someone's head, it's on! It's the perfect game for a hot summer day.

DUCK, DUCK, [NOUN]: The picker taps the ducks on the head, but instead of selecting the "goose," they shout out a random person or animal. Then, the pickee tries to catch the picker while both imitate whatever noun the picker shouted. For example, a frog hops, a horse gallops, and Godzilla might slowly and clumsily stomp around, breathing fire onto the other players.

FOWL FACTS

- Canada geese can be an invasive species. Sure, they look pretty when they're flying overhead in V formation, but the mess they leave behind is anything but beautiful. A Canada goose can defecate more than ninety times a day.

- Geese are socially monogamous creatures. Once they find a mate, they stick together for life.

- Canada geese fly in the shape of a V when they migrate. This saves energy—as the geese fly, the birds at the front of the V create an upward airstream, which helps lift the birds behind them, allowing them to expend less energy. The geese take turns leading. When the front-runner tires, it drops from the front of the V. Another goose then becomes the leader. Teamwork!

LUTEFISK

At Christmastime, Scandinavians pull out all the stops and offer up a dish like none other. Lutefisk is especially popular among Mid-westerners with Scandinavian heritage. In fact, more lutefisk is consumed in the United States than in Norway. It loosely translates to "lye fish," which is exactly what it is; salted, dried cod fish is rehydrated, and then soaked in lye until it becomes gelatinous, jellified, ammoni-ated, pungent fish goo. In Finland, lutefisk is made with birch ash instead of lye. The ash is high in potassium carbonate and bicarbonate, which gives it a much mellower flavor.

It is still awful!

Typically, lutefisk starts as a codfish, but really any whitefish will do. The fish is salted and dried, meaning it can be preserved for a long time before it is freakishly converted into a jelly fish. The dried fish is first soaked in water for about six days to soften it up. It's moved into a mixture of lye and water for about two days. The lye breaks down the proteins in the fish by about 50 percent. The remaining proteins hold the fish together, so breaking the others down gives the lutefisk its gelatinous texture.

At this point, you wouldn't want to eat the fish. The lye makes the fish extremely caustic, about 11 or 12 on the pH scale. "Caustic" means it can damage any surface it comes in contact with, in this case by chemically burning through that surface. You would not want it to burn through your stomach lining or your mouth. To make the fish safe to eat, it has to soak in clean water for about six more days. Finally, the lutefisk is ready to be cooked and eaten. Doesn't that sound tasty?

Oddly, the other 99 percent of the world also dries cod and other fish and they make some of

In Minnesota, we call it lute-ah-fisk, ya sure, you betcha!

the world's best dishes, like brandade or sautéed bacalao with tomatoes and white wine . . . but leave it to the Scandinavians to make putrid fish jelly out of it!

LutefiskTory

No one knows how the first lutefisk meal came to be. Some believe someone accidently dropped some fish into a lye bucket. Some believe it was a way to store fish for long periods outdoors. Others think it was just a practical joke that got out of hand.

Lutefisk was first documented in a sixteenth-century letter written by Swedish king Gustav I; however, folklore dates the dish waaaaaaaay further back. According to legend, lutefisk got its beginnings in Ireland, when the Vikings pillaged the Irish and wreaked havoc throughout the country. St. Patrick sent men to feed spoiled fish to the Vikings. They ended up enjoying the fish, so St. Patrick ordered the men to pour lye on the fish to poison the Vikings. It did not work.

Instead, the Vikings declared the lutefisk a delicacy. Of course, this is just a tall tale, as St. Patrick was in Ireland about three centuries before the Vikings ever got there.

"O LUTEFISK"

Sometimes when you eat lutefisk, you feel like singing. This song was written by Red Stangeland, in honor of the gelatinous fish. Sing it to the tune of "O Tannenbaum" ("O Christmas Tree" in English).

1. O Lutefisk, O Lutefisk, how fragrant your aroma,
   O Lutefisk, O Lutefisk, you put me in a coma.
   You smell so strong, you look like glue,
   You taste just like an overshoe,
   But lutefisk, come Saturday,
   I tink I eat you anyvay.

2. O Lutefisk, O Lutefisk, I put you in the doorvay.
   I wanted you to ripen up just like they do in Norvay.
   A dog came by and sprinkled you.
   I hit him with my overshoe.
   O Lutefisk, now I suppose
   I'll eat you while I hold my nose.

3. O Lutefisk, O Lutefisk, how well I do remember.
   On Christmas Eve how we'd receive
            our big treat of December.
   It wasn't turkey or fried ham.
   It wasn't even pickled SPAM.
   My mother knew there was no risk
   In serving buttered lutefisk.

4. O Lutefisk, O Lutefisk, now everyone discovers
   That lutefisk and lefse make Norwegians better lovers.
   Now all the world can have a ball.
   You're better than that Geritol.
   O Lutefisk, with brennevin [Norwegian brandy]
   You make me feel like Errol Flynn.

5. O Lutefisk, O Lutefisk, you have a special flavor.
   O Lutefisk, O Lutefisk, all good Norwegians savor.
   That slimy slab we know so well
   Identified by ghastly smell.
   O Lutefisk, O Lutefisk,
   Our loyalty won't waver.

OTHER USES FOR LYE

Lye, aka caustic soda, is a chemical called sodium hydroxide in science-speak. Besides turning fish to jelly, here are some other uses for lye (*not* to be ingested!):

CLEANING THE HAIR FROM THE SHOWER DRAIN
POWERING BATTERIES
HELPING DRILL FOR OIL
POLISHING ALUMINUM
KILLING WEEDS

Ewww!

SWedish Fish

Lutefisk is not the only Scandinavian gummy fish I love to eat. Malaco, a candy company that's been in business since 1958, makes my favorite: Swedish Fish. They might be shaped like fish, but they don't taste like them. The iconic fish is red with a flavor that is indiscernible to eaters; some think it's lingonberry, others cherry, others still think it's strawberry. Here are some more bizarre gummies.

GUMMY PIZZA

GUMMY BURGERS

GUMMY TONGUES

GUMMY BRAIN

GUMMY BACON

WORLD'S LARGEST GUMMY BEAR

GUMMY EGGS

Maggot Cheese

Picture it: You slice into a beautiful wheel of cheese. The perfectly aged rind, the pungent rotted diaper scent of coagulated milk, and your ears pick up the teeniest tiniest little squeak, the pitter-patter of little . . . maggots?

That's right, this midsized wheel of cheese is filled with wriggling and jiggling fly larvae. Maggot cheese, also called *casu marzu*, is an Italian delicacy most commonly found in the mountainous regions of northern Sardinia. You find similar cheeses in France, Germany, and Nicaragua. I

have tried them on two continents and absolutely adore the stuff. I'll bet most of you would agree with me if you tried it.

You'd think finding baby flies in your food would be a bad thing, but these maggots are purposely added to the cheese. *Piophila casei*, aka the cheese fly, loves laying its eggs in Pecorino cheese, which is made from sheep's milk. Once the eggs hatch, the larvae begin to chow down and digest the cheese, breaking down the fat and leaving behind a gloriously soft, runny decomposing center of an otherwise hard cheese comprised mostly of baby fly turds. The Sardinians call the oozy stuff in the middle of the roughly 2-kilo-sized wheels *lagrima*, which translates to "tears" in English.

Once you get a hold of maggot cheese, some of you have a decision to make. I guess there are people like me who go all-in for eating the 0.3-inch translucent white worms, but I have seen some opt for a larvae-free bite or two. With good *casu marzu*, there is no point in not eating the larvae. To pick them out would be akin to trying to pull the fat out of a wagyu steak—fruitless and illogical. When you do eat the maggots, be careful because they can be jumpy. The

Check out this gargantuan wheel of cheese, stuffed with writhing maggots. This Sardinian farm makes some of the best maggot cheese in the world.

HOW TO MAKE MAGGOT CHEESE

Step 1: Make a wheel of Pecorino cheese and place mature cheese wheel outdoors.

Step 2: Allow the *piophila casei*, or cheese fly, to lay eggs in cheese.

Step 3: Wait for the eggs to hatch and the larvae to begin eating the cheese. The cheese is ready for you to eat when it becomes soft and begins to weep its liquid-y goodness. But you won't see it through the hard aged exterior. Practice makes perfect.

maggots can fling themselves several inches in the air if they sense danger. The effete professional maggot-cheese eaters will eat thin slices of the cheese on Sardinian flatbread, making sure to hold their hands above the cheese, so their meal doesn't hop away. I just schmear big globs of the goopiest, runniest, most ammoniated nubbins of the stuff I can find onto crusty pieces of country bread and blissfully sigh my way to heaven. The stuff is that good.

BE WARNED: If you slice into your wheel of cheese and find the maggots are not moving, something is wrong with your cheese. If you want to try the cheese sans maggots, place your cheese in a paper bag. The maggots will jump around until they are starved of oxygen and you can pick them out of the cheese. However you choose to eat it, maggot cheese will be a meal to remember.

Where to Find Maggot Cheese

Though Sardinians have been cultivating this delicacy for hundreds of years, it can be hard to come by. If you want to sample *casu marzu*, you'll have to find it on the black market. Be prepared for the price tag. . . . It's very expensive (about two to three times the price of the same kind of cheese without maggots), and even if you think you've found a mountain shepherd selling it, you'll have to earn their trust. The cheese is kept under close wraps because those caught serving the delicacy are stuck with hefty fines.

BE WARNED, AGAIN

Although maggot cheese is a tasty treat, the maggots are resistant to stomach acid. This means the larvae can live inside of the human body for . . . a while. They have been known to attempt to bore through the stomach lining and internal organs. As you'd imagine, this causes serious problems. Maggot cheese was banned in Italy for some time and is currently banned in the United States.

FUNKY *PIOPHILA CASEI* FACTS

- The cheese fly is a scavenger insect, which means it looks for food in decomposing animal products and fungi.

- The cheese fly can help forensic scientists estimate a time of death. The flies do not take up residence in a corpse until three to six months after death.

- The larvae can jump 6 inches, which is twenty times their length. They jump by turning themselves into a spring. A larvae will curl itself up and grab its tail with its "mouth-hook." When the maggot tenses its muscles it will release its tail and pop up into the air.

- A female cheese fly can lay more than 500 eggs at one time.

This isn't maggot cheese, just a bowl full of maggots.

Who Cut the Cheese?

Beans aren't the only "musical fruit." Lots of other foods might lead to toots. The average person will fart, S.B.D. (Silent But Deadly) or otherwise, fourteen times per day. Where does all of that gas come from? Some of it is swallowed air, but the rest is the by-product of food broken down by bacteria in the digestive system. Some foods are more notorious than others for producing thunder down under. Sugary foods tend to be the culprit more often than not and foods high in fiber will just increase the stench.

The official name for the gas released in a fart is called "flatus." Flatus is made up of oxygen, nitrogen, hydrogen, carbon dioxide, and the stinker, methane. But every once in a while, a chemical reaction occurs creating hydrogen sulfide, which has a smell reminiscent of rotten eggs.

Just remember this wise idiom before you ask, "Who cut the cheese?": He who smelt it dealt it.

Other Fart Names

Backfire • Stepping on a duck • Butt tuba • Cut muffins • Drop a bomb • Fannitosis • Mating call of the barking spider • Start a Harley • Message from the Interior • Speak German • Trouser cough • Bean fumes • Atmosphere of Uranus • Rip the canvas • Toot • Shoot bunnies • After-dinner mint

LIMBURGER: The Other Noxious Cheese

And now for a cheese that has a funk all its own. Known as the stinkiest of them all, Limburger cheese was first produced in 1867 in the Duchy of Limburg—an area that is now parts of Belgium, the Netherlands, and Germany. Today, the cheese is mostly found in Germany, but the only North American companies that make this cheese are the Williams Cheese Company in Linwood, Michigan, and the Chalet Cheese Cooperative in Monroe, Wisconsin.

For the last century and a half, this dairy product has assaulted the noses of folks around the globe. So what gives this food its pungent scent? Three months of fermentation that encourages bacteria, the same stuff that causes body odor on human skin, to grow like a weed.

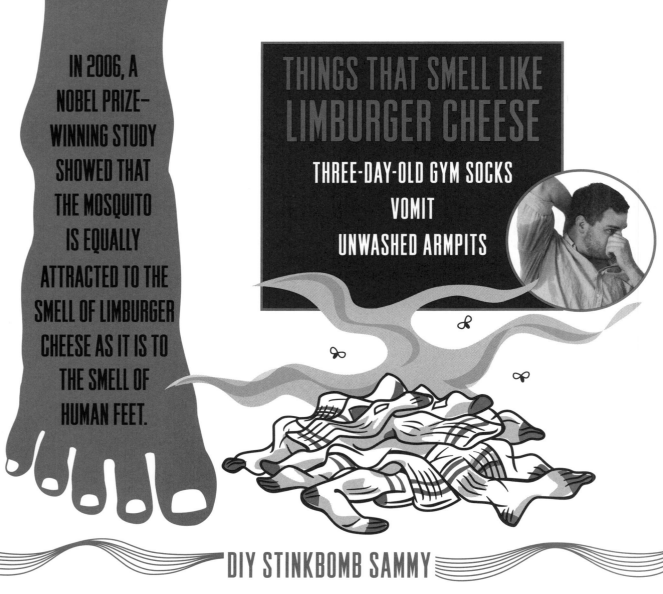

IN 2006, A NOBEL PRIZE-WINNING STUDY SHOWED THAT THE MOSQUITO IS EQUALLY ATTRACTED TO THE SMELL OF LIMBURGER CHEESE AS IT IS TO THE SMELL OF HUMAN FEET.

THINGS THAT SMELL LIKE LIMBURGER CHEESE

THREE-DAY-OLD GYM SOCKS

VOMIT

UNWASHED ARMPITS

DIY STINKBOMB SAMMY

Limburger sandwiches were very popular among German immigrants in the Midwest, but they've become increasingly hard to find because of the cheese's stench. Restaurants and delis find it hard to keep the cheese with the smell. Kraft used to make a Limburger cheese spread, but it has been discontinued.

If you want to try this lunch treat, your best bet is to do it yourself. First, shmear the soft Limburger cheese on a slice of rye bread. Top with a slice of raw onion and brown mustard. Top with another piece of rye. Best served with black coffee or a beer, with a side of toothbrush and toothpaste for the funky-mouth-stench aftermath.

OCTOPUS (live ones!)

Sannakji is a Korean dish made of octopus, but that isn't even the weird part. The weird part is watching your still-wiggling dinner try to walk off your plate. The *nakji*, which means "small octopus" in Korean, are typically cut into small pieces right before serving. Though the animal is dead, electrical impulses still in the octopus's arms cause the pieces to move around until they're eaten. Sometimes even after that.

Octopus can be very chewy, and it is important to remember to chew sannakji very well. The suction cups on the octopus arms are still active and will try to grab on to your throat. Live octopus can be a challenging meal to eat, but Koreans claim an octopus-rich diet increases your strength and stamina. It's typically eaten with both sesame oil to help it slide down, and salt, which makes it writhe around a bit more. This proves that even in the kitchen, for every action there is an equal and opposite reaction.

OCTOPUS FUN FACTS

Getting ready to dig into octopus in Mexico.

- The octopus is a cephalopod. It gets its name from its eight suction-cup-covered arms. (*Octopus* means "eight-footed" in Greek.)

- The octopus has a beak that looks similar to a parrot's. Because it is the only hard part in the octopus's body, it can squeeze into very small spaces to avoid predators.

- All octopi are venomous, but only the blue-ringed octopus is deadly to humans.

- They have three hearts; one pumps blood to the whole body, the other two pump blood to each of its gills.

- Octopi have multiple tactics for avoiding predators, including camouflage, the expulsion of ink, hiding, and bursts of speed. While it might seem like ink blocks a predator's vision, it actually dulls their sense of smell, which large sea predators rely on to catch their prey.

- They have excellent short-term and long-term memory. Studies have shown they can remember shapes and patterns.

- A female octopus will lay around 50,000 eggs. She will care for the eggs while they are developing (around forty days) by blowing oxygen on them and protecting them from predators. Since a mother octopus cannot leave her eggs alone, she will eat one of her own arms to sustain her.

- As a mother octopus's eggs hatch, she blows them out of her den and they swim to the surface. They float with plankton for a few months and eventually sink to the bottom to live as adults.

- When an octopus's blood is exposed to air it turns blue.

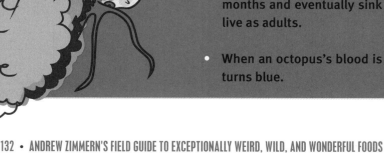

- Octopi have short lives, typically around two years. Males will die a few months after mating, and the female will die shortly after her eggs hatch.

- An octopus does not have the neurological pathways to tell where its arms are and what they are doing. In order to control its movement, the octopus must watch its arms to see where they are and what they are doing.

- As a decoy, octopi will sometimes lose one of their arms to avoid a predator. They will regrow in six to eight weeks.

- In order to camouflage itself, an octopus has special cells that reflect the color of the surface it is hiding on. The octopus can also control the texture and pattern of those cells.

Baby octopi. Cute, aren't they?

LiKE a CHiCKEN WitH Its HEaD CUt OFF...

As I mentioned earlier, a recently slaughtered octopus will continue to wiggle its arms long after it's dead as a doornail. This happens with other animals, too. There is an expression "like a chicken with its head cut off." Chickens have been known to run around after they have been decapitated because they still have electrical impulses through their bodies. This happens with humans also. But we won't go there.

On September 10, 1945, Clara Olsen of Fruita, Colorado, planned on turning one of her five-and-a-half-month-old Wyandotte roosters into dinner. She sent her husband, Lloyd Olsen, to slaughter the rooster. He had to decapitate it, but his mother-in-law was joining them for supper. Lloyd knew the neck was his mother-in-law's favorite part, so he tried to leave a bit more on the chicken. He chopped off the chicken's head . . . but the chicken didn't die. Mike, as the chicken was named, would peck at food and preen his feathers. When the Olsens realized that Mike was going to keep living, they figured out that they could feed him and give him water through an eyedropper. The Olsens took Mike to the University of Utah in Salt Lake City to find out more about why he lived. Lloyd Olsen's ax had missed Mike's jugular vein, and a blood clot prevented him from bleeding to death. Most of Mike's brain stem and one ear were still attached to his body. Mike lived eighteen months after his head was cut off. He began to choke and the Olsens could not find the eyedropper to clear his throat. The town of Fruita celebrates Mike's headless life every year on the third weekend in May.

Other Octos

OCTOMOM: Nadya Suleman was dubbed the "Octomom" by the media after she gave birth to octuplets (eight babies) in January 2009.

OCTOBER: Although October is the tenth month of the year, it is named October because it was the eighth month on the Roman calendar. October is also the month of World Food Day (October 16).

THE OCTAGON: Ultimate Fighting Championship is a mixed martial arts company. Fighters step into the "Octagon" to see who will come out on top. UFC fighters use a variety of martial arts in their fights from Greco-Roman wrestling to kickboxing to kung fu.

DOC OCK: Doctor Octopus, Spider-Man's multi-limbed nemisis.

OCTOGENARIANS: Anyone from the age of eighty to eighty-nine is an octogenarian. Famous octogenarians include Bob Barker from *The Price Is Right* and Stan Lee, the comic-book writer who created *Spider-Man*, *X-Men*, *The Fantastic Four*, *Iron Man,* and *The Hulk*.

Stan Lee

OCTOPUSSY: In the thirteenth entry in the series, Roger Moore plays the ever-suave James Bond on the trail of a jewel smuggler . . . who just so happens to be a hot, leggy brunette. Don't look at me—I didn't come up with her name!

OX HEART

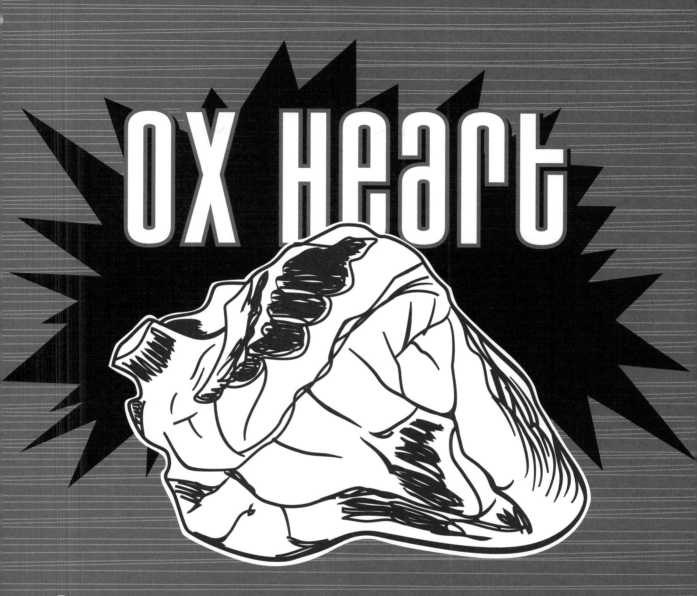

♥ ox heart. It's lean, since it's almost pure muscle, with very little fat and collagen. And coming in at around two pounds apiece, ox heart is offal-y large. It tastes like beef, which makes sense because oxen are cattle that have been trained as draft animals. Oxen are usually eaten after the ox can no longer perform its drafting duties. Despite its meaty flavor, ox can also have a pronounced gamey taste, but the heart is splendidly beefy. Sliced thin, grilled over hot wood charcoal until charred rare, and served under a tangle of olive oil– and lemon-dressed arugula, it's one of my favorite foods.

WHAT EXACTLY IS AN OX?

- An ox is a bovine that has been trained as a draft animal. If it hasn't been trained for manual labor, it is just cattle.

- A draft animal is an animal that has been trained by humans to perform a task. For example, a dog that has been trained to guide the blind or a camel that is trained as a transport. In the case of an ox, the animal is typically trained to pull carts or plows.

- Oxen are typically male cattle that have been castrated, but can also be bulls (male cattle that have not been castrated) or female cattle.

- An ox is called a "bullock" in Australia, New Zealand, and India.

- As draft animals, oxen typically work in pairs. Each pair is often given names that "go together," sort of like Santa's reindeer: Dasher and Dancer, Prancer and Vixen, Comet and Cupid, and Donner and Blitzen.

Take a whole, fresh ox heart. Slice it up, sprinkle with salt and pepper, grill for a few minutes, and voilà! Some of the best eatin' on the animal, if you ask me.

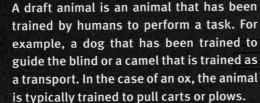

HOW to Direct an OX

In order for a draft animal to help get a job done, it needs to be able to take directions. An ox driver, also called a "teamster" or a "bullocky," usually uses a goad (a whip or a rod) and verbal cues to direct the oxen. Here are a few in case you ever find yourself behind the wheel (or reins) of an oxen-drawn cart:

Get up: go
Whoa: stop
Back up: back up
Gee: turn to the right
Haw: turn to the left

Your Heart

Every animal with a circulatory system has a heart. It acts as a pump, pushing 2,000 gallons of blood through our body every day, just as an example. With its four compartments, the heart keeps "thump-thumping" its own electrical impulse. That sound is the valves in the heart opening and closing. An adult male's heart will beat about seventy times per minute, while an adult female's beats about seventy-eight times per minute. That leads to about 100,000 times in one day, 35 million times in one year, and about 2.5 billion beats in the average lifetime. The heart sits in the center of the chest leaning slightly to the left to make room for the lungs. From there, it pumps blood through 60,000 miles of blood vessels per day, some as large as a garden hose like the aorta artery and some as thin as human hair like some capillaries.

Heart as a Symbol

The heart is a symbol for love. Before modern medicine, it was believed the heart was where humans thought, so emotions were often linked to the heart. Now we know better, but the stylized red heart is still used on Valentine's Day and at the end of love letters to show someone we care. In fact, we use the heart to symbolize love so often, we've developed an emoticon for it. Emoticons are pictorial representations of a facial expression or shape. Here are a few to use when you're sending text messages:

<3 | Heart

:-) | Happy face

D: | Horror

;-) | Winking face

:'-(| Crying

@}-;-'— | Rose

:B | Buck-tooth

:-9 | Licking chops/just ate ox heart

(:^9) | Andrew Zimmern

Captain Beefheart

Captain Beefheart was a "blues-rock" musician known for his powerful voice. Don Van Vliet, his real name, began his music career in 1964. He performed with The Magic Band and Frank Zappa, singing and playing numerous instruments, including saxophone and harmonica. As you can tell by his unique name, Beefheart was a performer. He claimed he had never read a book and had never been to school. He retired from music in 1982 and pursued a career as an artist.

Rabbit

There's a hare in my soup! Oh, wait. It's supposed to be there. Found on tables in the Americas, Europe, and parts of the Middle East, rabbit and hare are just as cute as they are delicious. Rabbit meat is most often categorized into three groups. Fryer cuts come from rabbits up to nine weeks in age and between four and five pounds, and render a tender, fine-grained meat. Roaster cuts come from rabbits over five pounds and are usually firm and coarse. The last category of rabbit meat is giblets, also known as the internal organs like the heart and liver. Giblets is a much cuter name.

Most rabbit served in restaurants comes from farms. Frankly, I am surprised there aren't more of them in the United States. High in protein, relatively low in cholesterol and calories (less than chicken and turkey), rabbit both tastes great and is good for you. It's very versatile, too: Where you can use chicken, you can use rabbit.

ROASTED RABBIT WITH ORANGE AND FENNEL

I love rabbit. Here is a great recipe.

1 large rabbit, cut into sixths, roughly 4½ pounds
Kosher salt and pepper
Flour for dredging
4 tablespoons olive oil
⅔ cup sherry wine vinegar
3 cups homemade rich chicken stock

2 medium-sized fennel bulbs, trimmed
3 cups peeled and sliced carrots
1 cup fresh-squeezed orange juice
½ cup cooked and cooled peas
1 orange, peeled and segmented, freed of all connective tissue and filament

- Preheat oven to 350°.

- Season the rabbit with the salt and pepper and dredge with the flour; discard excess.

- Place the olive oil in large Dutch oven over medium-high heat and brown the rabbit pieces very well. Remove rabbit and reserve.

- Add the vinegar, scraping the pan, reduce by half.

- Add the stock and reduce by one-third.

- Return the rabbit to the pan, cover, and braise in the oven for one hour.

- Slice the fennel lengthwise into sixths.

- Uncover the rabbit, add the carrots, fennel, and orange juice.

- Raise temperature to 400° and cook uncovered for another 20–25 minutes; skim the sauce.

- Reserve the meat and vegetables to a platter, return the pan to medium heat on your stove top, and reduce liquids to sauce consistency. Add peas and oranges to pot, season, pour sauce over rabbit, and serve.

EXPAND YOUR VOCABULARY!

CUNICULTURIST: a fancy name for one who breeds and raises rabbits.

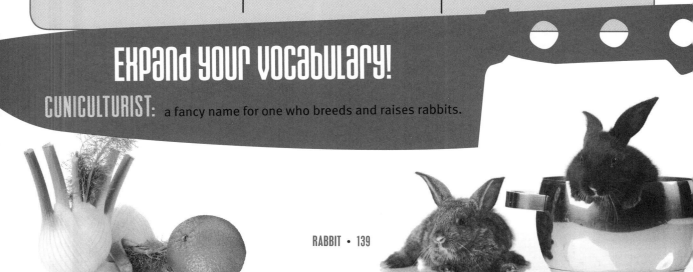

Rabbit FUN Facts

- All rabbits originated from North America. They were brought to different parts of the world as a food source. They quickly became a pesty species, reproducing quickly and devastating crops.

- The different species of rabbit live in different habitats. The most well-known species of rabbit is the European rabbit that lives in burrows, known as rabbit holes.

- A rabbit's ears can be as long as a dozen inches and were most likely adapted for detecting predators. Because rabbits are prey animals (and completely delicious, by the way), they must be aware of their surroundings at all times.

- Rabbits' eyes are positioned high on their heads so they have nearly 360-degree vision.

- The jackrabbit can run at about 45 miles per hour.

- When being chased, rabbits run in a zigzag motion. This makes it more difficult for predators to follow the rabbit's scent.

- When a rabbit senses danger, it often pauses and will then pound the ground with its powerful hind leg. This serves as a warning signal to the other rabbits underground in their burrows.

- Rabbits have an epiglottis that covers their soft palate except when they swallow. This means rabbits only breathe through their noses.

- Rabbits eat a large amount of cellulose, which is found in plants and grasses, but can be difficult to digest. To aid digestion, rabbits have two types of feces: hard pellets and soft black pellets. When the rabbits pass the soft pellets, they eat them and let them go through digestion once again. And you thought my diet was strange.

- Rabbits are able to reproduce at a rapid rate. Where a human's gestation period is about nine months, a rabbit's is only about thirty days. Rabbits can also have four to twelve kits or kittens (baby rabbits) in one litter. In one breeding season, which lasts from February to October (nine months), one rabbit can produce up to 800 children, grandchildren, and great-grandchildren.

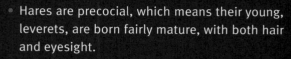

WHAT'S THE DIFFERENCE: RABBIT AND HARE?

- Rabbits and hares come from the same order, Lagomorpha. The most distinct difference between rabbits and hares is that rabbits are altricial. "Altricial" means "needing nourishment." Altricial animals cannot travel right after being born. For example, a human baby has to be carried around, whereas a baby horse can get up and walk minutes after being born. Altricial animals are often hairless and blind (either their eyes have not fully developed or they keep their eyes closed).

- Hares are precocial, which means their young, leverets, are born fairly mature, with both hair and eyesight.

- All rabbits, except for the cottontail rabbit, live in groups in underground burrows called warrens.

- Hares and the cottontail rabbit live in nests aboveground and do not live in groups.

- Physically, hares are larger than rabbits, with larger ears. They also typically have black markings in their fur.

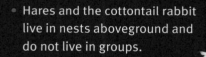

The Easter Bunny

A rabbit often symbolizes fertility and new life. The Easter bunny goes along with the idea of new life and spring. The Easter bunny began in Germany, where good children were left colored eggs. Coloring eggs came from ancient Egypt, Persia, Greece, and Rome, where eggs were dyed and given as gifts to celebrate the coming of spring.

In addition to eggs, the Easter bunny often leaves a chocolate version of himself. Ninety million chocolate bunnies are produced each year. The edible Easter bunny tradition comes from Germany, where they would dole out pastry bunnies on Easter.

Chocolate bunnies became popular in the United States around 1890 after a Pennsylvania drugstore owner named Robert L. Strohecker put a 5-foot-tall chocolate rabbit in his window as an Easter promotion. If you think that's big, the world's largest chocolate bunny was made in South Africa by an artist named Harry Johnson. The rabbit was 12 feet, 5 inches tall.

What part of a chocolate bunny do you eat first? According to the National Confectioners Association, a survey of 1,000 adults showed that 76 percent start with the ears. Eating bunnies' feet first (5 percent) and tail first (4 percent) were left in the dust.

BUNNIES CAN BE WEIRD—AND CREEPY. PROOF:

HARVEY (1950): Delusional man has an invisible 6-foot-tall bunny as a bestie? Totally, 100-percent terrifying.

DONNIE DARKO (2001): Frank, a demonic rabbit, haunted Donnie Darko . . . and every other human being that ever saw that frightful movie.

THE VAMPIRE RABBIT OF NEWCASTLE: This blood-covered beast overlooks the St. Nicholas Cathedral. With its bloody canine teeth, sharp claws, and sinister eyes, it's much scarier than a gargoyle, don't you think?

FATAL ATTRACTION (1987): Psychotic Glenn Close sends a message to her former lovah (played by Michael Douglas) by boiling his daughter's pet rabbit. Needless to say, that message is not one of good tidings.

MONTY PYTHON AND THE HOLY GRAIL (1974): Foul and cruel with a vicious streak a mile wide, the Killer Rabbit of Caerbannog gnaws its prey into bloody bits. Run away!

WHO FRAMED ROGER RABBIT? (1988): Not sure what's creepier—the dark, grim side of Toontown or the fact that Roger Rabbit's wife, Jessica, is a good-lookin' gal in a painted-on dress . . . like, for real.

ENERGIZER BUNNY: Why won't this thing stop?!

TRIX RABBIT: An anthropomorphic rabbit that literally steals candy from babies. It's almost too much to take.

JACKALOPE: A jackrabbit mixed with an antelope. Bizarre!

LUCKY CHARMS

Some people believe carrying a rabbit's foot around with them can be good luck. Like most superstitions, its origin is a little sketchy. Linked to the pre-Celtic people living in Britain around 600 BC, young hunters would be presented the foot of the first rabbit they killed in a ceremony welcoming them into manhood.

Need some luck but don't want to carry around a rabbit's foot? Here are some other lucky charms to try:

LADYBUGS:
Actually called ladybird beetles, the ladybug is a symbol of luck. The more spots, the luckier it is. According to folklore, if a man and woman see a ladybug at the same time, they will fall in love.

FOUR-LEAF CLOVERS:
An Irish symbol for good luck. They are hard to come by, which might insinuate luck if you find one. The four leaves represent faith, hope, love, and luck.

HORSESHOES:
Legend says that Saint Dunstan, a blacksmith, nailed a horseshoe to the devil's foot. The devil guaranteed he would stay away from any house with a horseshoe on the door.

SHOOTING STAR:
While you can't keep a shooting star in your pocket, seeing one is good luck. You can make a wish, and it will come true! (Note: Wishing on an airplane or satellite will not give you good luck.)

GOLDFISH:
According to feng shui, goldfish attract luck and prosperity. Many people will keep goldfish in ponds outside of their homes for good luck.

POLTERABEND:
This pre-wedding German tradition involves the bride and groom's best friends and family gathering for the sole purpose of breaking loads of plates, cups, toilets—anything ceramic—and watching the engaged couple clean it up. This is supposed to symbolize working together in a marriage, but in reality it sounds like a fantastically fun and destructive event for everyone (except the cleaner-uppers).

Rat

I have eaten quite a few rats in my day, and I'm here to tell you they are pretty darn tasty. Bush and pack rats of several species in Arizona, jungle rats of several types in Ecuador and Suriname, Royal rats (gibnuts) in Belize, cane rats in Uganda, rice rats in Thailand, a giant rat that reminded me of aguti in Cuba . . . even a crazy giant aquatic rodent called a nutria in Louisiana—they are all rats of various sizes and nothing (except bats and blood) does more to prove my point that eating preferences and picky eater syndrome are learned behaviors that can be unlearned than my enjoyment of rats.

In our country we are obsessed with the cultural messaging that rat is an evil meat, diseased and unclean like the animals themselves. And here in our country it's mostly true. But like any other food animal, in many places that is not the case. A simple glance at a cow will tell you if it is sick or not, so you don't eat one that is obviously afflicted. Same with rat. I can't even look at them in New York City while waiting for the subway at midnight, but a 20-pound forest rat in the jungles of South America is a glorious beast. Rats like that one feed mostly on fallen date palms and other fruit and have the succulent sweet flavor that I associate more with pork shoulder than with any other meat.

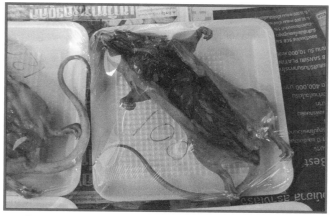

In Thailand, rat is skinned, gutted, and ready for your home grill.

RAT FACTS

Our hatred of rats, bats, and other oddities is as much psychological as it is practical, and with so much disinformation out there in the ether, I thought it best to offer a primer on the noble rat, for better or worse.

There are fifty-one different species of these medium-sized, long-tailed rodents. Their scientific name is *Rattus*, although some rodents commonly called "rats" do not come from the *Rattus* family—they just look like rats. Rats are commensals, which means they benefit from living near another animal. So, what animal does the rat like to scrounge off of? Humans. It makes sense if you think about it. Humans leave a lot of food lying around—crumbs, leftover grains, pizza crusts. All

the rats have to do is wait for a restaurant to throw out the day's trash and they have a smorgasbord of fresh vegetables and meat scraps. Although they have poor eyesight, rats use their excellent sense of smell to find food.

Despite their negative image, rats are actually very caring creatures. Rats hang out in a group called a "mischief," which is a tight-knit clan. Rats will take care of fellow ill and injured rats.

They also make for very loving pets. Jack Black (no, not the actor Jack Black) was the name of Queen Victoria of England's royal rat catcher in the 1860s. He caught an albino rat in a graveyard and bred the first albino rats in captivity. Beatrix Potter, the author of *The Tale of Peter Rabbit*, took one of those rats in as her pet.

RAT • 145

The Karni Devi Temple

According to legend, after a young Indian boy died, his parents prayed to the goddess Devi to revive him. Devi went to retrieve the boy's soul only to find he had already been reincarnated into the body of a rat. Devi vowed that the souls of the Charan clan would be placed in the bodies of rats until they could be reincarnated back into the clan. To this day, the Karni Devi Temple in India is filled with rats, where they are treated with respect and well fed. It's believed that the rats harbor the souls of the Charan clan waiting to be reincarnated.

You Dirty Rat

The Black Death gave rats a bad name. The pandemic was caused by the bubonic plague, a bacterium called *Yersinia pestis*. This was no ordinary "bug"; it was responsible for the death of 30 to 60 percent of Europe's population during the mid-1300s. The world's population went from 450 million people to between 350 and 375 million people. Many people blamed rats for causing the plague, but it was actually caused by the fleas that carry the bacterium that would travel on the rats' backs. Rats became notorious for being dirty animals, but in reality they are very clean. They spend hours a day cleaning themselves. You are more likely to get sick from a dog or cat than a rat.

Rat Pack

As the story goes, American actor Humphrey Bogart and a group of friends came home from a trip to Las Vegas looking worn and tired. Bogart's wife, actress Lauren Bacall, saw her husband and his mangy-looking group and said they looked like a "[blankety-blank] rat pack." And the name Rat Pack was born. The original group consisted of Bacall, Bogart, and other big Hollywood names like Judy Garland and big music stars like Frank Sinatra. Members joined and left the group, but after Bogart passed away in 1957, the group stopped calling themselves the Rat Pack. This did not deter the media from picking up the name. They attached it to a group of five performers known for being pals on and off movie sets: Frank Sinatra (part of the original Rat Pack), Dean Martin, Sammy Davis Jr., Peter Lawford, and Joey Bishop. The Rat Pack was very popular in the 1960s. If one member had a show, other members would show up for surprise appearances, drawing in large crowds. They also starred in many films together, including the original *Ocean's Eleven* and *The Cannonball Run*.

The Rat Pack: Lawford, Martin, Davis, Sinatra.

Pied Piper of Hamelin

In this German fairy tale, rats were overrunning the German town of Hamelin. The townspeople hired the Pied Piper to lure the rats away from the town with his magical pipe. ("Pied" means "multicolored" and it refers to his colorful attire.) The piper said he could get rid of the rats and the townspeople said they would pay him for it. He played his magical pipe and the rats followed him. He led the rats to a river to drown. All the rats drowned except for one, who wandered back into the town. The townspeople told the piper they would not pay him. He did not get rid of *all* the rats, so they did not need to keep up their end of the bargain. The piper left the town stating he would come back to seek revenge. One Sunday, while the townspeople were in church, the piper returned and began playing his pipe. Soon the town's children followed him. He led the children out of the town and they were never seen again.

The moral of the story: Pay the piper.

RATS VS. MICE

- Both mice and rats are rodents, but they are from different genera.

- "Rat" and "mouse" are not scientific names, so they generally describe characteristics seen by the naked eye.

- Rats are much larger than mice. Rats usually weigh about a pound, whereas mice are only a few ounces.

- Rats have longer muzzles and thick tails.

- In ancient Rome, mice were considered a type of rat. They were called Rattus Minor ("little rat") while the rats we know today were called Rattus Major ("big rat").

RATATOUILLE

Perhaps made most well known from the 2007 Pixar/Disney film by the same name, ratatouille is a French dish that does *not* contain rat meat. In fact, the dish does not contain any meat at all. It is a stewed vegetable dish, most often served as a side. The name comes from the French word *touiller,* which means "to toss food."

Pack Rat

A pack rat is a term for someone who does not get rid of their things once they are no longer needed. For example, a pack rat might hang on to newspapers that have no historical or personal importance that are years old. This can range from keeping a few things to compulsive hoarding.

A pack rat is also a type of rodent that looks like a rat. They build nests, so they collect any material they find that might be helpful for nest building. Thus, the name pack rat.

scrapple

It's everything but the oink. Scrapple is a mush made of pork scraps and trimmings, cornmeal, flour, buckwheat flour, and spices. The ingredients are mixed up and turned into a semi-solid congealed loaf. Pan-fry the "meatloaf" until browned, and there you have it: scrapple. The scraps in scrapple are the pig head, pork heart, liver, and the rest of the organs. It's the perfect breakfast food to go along with some eggs and toast.

Scrapple was first created in the United States by the Pennsylvania Dutch, who called the dish *pon haus*. The Pennsylvania Dutch are not actually Dutch at all. The name comes from Deutsch, which is German for "German." The Pennsylvania Dutch were German farmers who settled in the Pennsylvania area. Around the seventeenth and eighteenth centuries, the colonists in the Philadelphia, Pennsylvania, area came up with the recipe for *pon haus*. The recipe was based on a Low German dish called *panhas*. It was slightly altered to make use of local ingredients.

Apple-Scrapple Festival

Every year in Bridgeville, Delaware, the town celebrates the Apple-Scrapple Festival. Bridgeville has been the home to RAPA Scrapple, the most well-known scrapple brand, since 1926. Ralph and Paul Adams, two brothers, created RAPA Scrapple to mass-produce their beloved dish. They combined the first two letters of their names to create the name RAPA. Their scrapple has been celebrated with events like a Miss and Little Miss Apple-Scrapple contest, a ladies' skillet toss, the mayor's scrapple sling, and a scrapple chuckin' contest, where contestants see who can throw a package of scrapple "shot-put style" the farthest.

Can't make it to Bridgeville? Have your own ode to scrapple with these scrapple games:

- Bobbing for scrapple. Fill a tub with water, drop in some scrapple, tie hands behind your back, start bobbin'!

- Roll scrapple into large meatballs. Play scrapple bocce ball in your backyard.

- Form a bunch of animal sculptures out of scrapple. Have a scrapple petting zoo!

scrabble

Scrapple is not to be confused with Scrabble, which is a word board game. Scrabble is sold in 121 countries in 29 different languages. An architect named Alfred Mosher Butts created the game in 1938. The game wasn't very popular until 1952, when the president of Macy's, Jack Strauss, played the game on vacation. When he got back, he was surprised that his store did not carry the game and he then made a large order. When the game found its way to Macy's its popularity took off. Since then Scrabble went through a number of owners and is currently owned by Hasbro. "Scrabble" is a real word, which means "to scratch frantically." That means you could throw that on the board for some serious points. The highest possible scoring word in Scrabble is "sesquioxidizing," which would be 2,015 points if it was covering triple word scores. Next time you play, remember the word "scrapple." It would be worth 14 points (S-1), (C-3), (R-1), (A-1), (P-3), (P-3), (L-1), (E-1).

The National Scrabble Association says that it's often easier to learn great words to whip out during Scrabble play if there is a theme. Here's a list of fantastic food words.

BABA	n	pl.	-S	a rum cake	CIBOL	n	pl.	-S	a variety of onion
BANGER	n	pl.	-S	a sausage	COMFIT	n	pl.	-S	a candy
BAP	n	pl.	-S	a small bun or roll	DUFF	n	pl.	-S	a thick pudding
BIFFIN	n	pl.	-S	a cooking apple	FAVA	n	pl.	-S	a bean
BREWIS	n	pl.	BREWISES	a broth	GUMBO	n	pl.	-S	the okra plant
PONE	n	pl.	-S	a corn bread	KALE	n	pl.	-S	a variety of cabbage
RUSK	n	pl.	-S	a sweetened biscuit	LICHI	n	pl.	-S	a Chinese fruit
SCONE	n	pl.	-S	a flat, round cake	ORZO	n	pl.	-S	a rice-shaped pasta
SPELT	n	pl.	-S	a variety of wheat	PILAF	n	pl.	-S	a rice dish
WHEY	n	pl.	-S	the watery part of milk	PINOT	n	pl.	-S	a red or white grape
YAM	n	pl.	-S	an edible plant root	SLOE	n	pl.	-S	a plumlike fruit
ZITI	n	pl.	-S	a tubular pasta	TOFU	n	pl.	-S	a soybean milk food

Pennsylvania Faves

Scrapple is just one of many iconic Pennsylvanian foods. Here are some of my other favorites:

HERSHEY CHOCOLATE: Every Hershey's bar comes from Pennsylvanian roots. Milton S. Hershey started making chocolate in Lancaster, Pennsylvania, after visiting the 1893 World's Columbian Exposition in Chicago. Before Hershey's he had been making the less iconic Lancaster Caramel Company. Today, Hershey has been put on the map, literally. Hershey built a town around his factory to create a strong community for his employees and their families.

SOFT PRETZELS: In AD 610, an Italian monk was making bread and decided to use his extra dough to create something special for his students. The pretzel's twist symbolized hands crossed on the chest in prayer. The pretzels made their way to Germany. When a group of Germans came to the United States and settled in Pennsylvania, they brought the pretzel with them.

SHOOFLY PIE: Another Pennsylvania Dutch dish, shoofly pie is a fluffy molasses pie. The molasses can attract flies that you have to "shoo" away, thus the name "shoofly."

POTATO CHIPS: Potato chips got their beginnings in New York after a disgruntled patron sent back his potatoes so many times that the chef decided to thinly slice the potatoes and fry them to a crisp with some salt. Since then, three major chip companies have been founded in the United States, two of which, Utz and Wise Foods, are located in Pennsylvania.

CHEESESTEAKS: Cheesesteaks were created by two Philadelphians, Pat and Harry Olivieri, in the 1930s. They started serving the steak sandwiches at their hot-dog stand. Today, you can't go to Philly without getting a delicious cheesesteak.

D. G. YUENGLING'S BEER: In 1829, David G. Yuengling built the Eagle Brewery in Pottsville, Pennsylvania. It is the oldest brewery in the United States. From 1919 to 1933, it was illegal in the United States to produce and consume alcohol. To survive Prohibition, Yuengling opened a dairy across the street from the brewery and started producing "near beer," a nonalcoholic beer, in the brewery.

PIEROGI: Originally from Poland, pierogi are baked or fried dumplings stuffed with potato filling, sauerkraut, ground meat, cheese, or fruit.

STROMBOLI: A turnover filled with cheeses, meat, and vegetables coming from Romano's Italian Restaurant in Essington, Tinicum Township, outside of Philadelphia in 1950. The name came from the Ingrid Bergman movie *Stromboli*.

APPLE PANDOWDY: A baked fruit dessert with sweet cake dough on top, it's featured in a song about Pennsylvania Dutch cooking by Guy Wood and Sammy Gallop called "Shoo-Fly Pie and Apple Pan Dowdy."

SOUR LUNG SOUP

S our Lung Soup is a German dish, most popular in Bavaria. In German, the dish is called *saure Lüngerl*, which translates to "sour (or acidic) lungs." Oddly enough, the dish isn't technically a soup at all. Finely sliced veal offal—such as lung, heart, and sweetbreads—is placed in a bowl and smothered in a sauce made of vinegar, sour cream, and parsley with bread dumplings.

The name "sour lung soup" may sound gross, but the stuff reminds me of borscht, an Eastern European sweet and sour cabbage soup. Sour lung soup is one of my favorite dishes in the whole world. The lungs shred up like cabbage or veggies, and because it's not a muscle mass, there is no fat. Fat is the place where off-tasting flavors thrive, so soup made with lung is very clean and delicious.

Lungs, also called "lights" by the British, contain a little more protein than a T-bone steak, but only 6 percent as much fat.

YOUR LUNGS

An essential organ for air-breathing animals, the lungs' main function is to bring oxygen from the air into the bloodstream and to take carbon dioxide out of the bloodstream.

Most mammals have two lungs, which are soft and spongy. Human lungs are located on either side of the heart, separated by lobes. Although the lungs look similar, they are not identical. The right lung has three lobes, whereas the left has two. The left lung is smaller to make room for the part of the heart that sits on the left side of the chest.

The word "lung" comes from the Old English word *lunge*, which means "light." This is because lungs are a very light (as in not heavy) organ. This is also why lungs are sometimes called lights. They are so light, they are the only organ that will float in water.

There are 1,500 miles of airways in the lungs, which helps since the average human takes 22,000 breaths every twenty-four hours. Women and children tend to have a faster breathing rate than men, which means they might be taking even more breaths in a day.

It is possible to live with just one lung. Because you would not be getting as much oxygen it can limit physical activity, but people with one lung can live relatively normal lives.

HOFBRÄUHAUS

The Hofbräuhaus is a well-known brewery in Germany. Its full name is the Staatliches Hofbräuhaus in München, which means "the state court-brewery in Munich."

The Hofbräuhaus was founded in 1589 by Wilhelm V., Duke of Bavaria, as the brewery to the old royal residence. Wilhelm V. disliked the beer in Germany, so his royal court recommended the state open their own brewery. The brewery's first brewer, Heimeran Pongratz, made the Hofbräuhaus beer world famous. The Bavarian Beer Purity Law of 1516 also helped. It stated that only natural ingredients could be used in the brewing process.

In 1632, the Hofbräuhaus beer saved Munich. During the Thirty Years' War, King Gustavus Adolphus of Sweden invaded Bavaria, threatening to burn down Munich. He left the city alone because the citizens agreed to surrender some hostages and gave Adolphus 600,000 barrels of Hofbräuhaus beer.

In 1828, the Hofbräuhaus was opened to commoners under the decree of King Ludwig I. In the nineteenth century, the Hofbräuhaus was

The original Hofbräuhaus beer hall in Munich, Germany.

converted into a large beer hall, restaurant, and place for entertainment. The Hofbräuhaus has a rich history. It has been visited by many historical figures, including Wolfgang Amadeus Mozart and John F. Kennedy. The Hofbräuhaus was swept up into political history around World War I. Lenin was a regular visitor to the brewery in the time he lived in Munich, in 1919 the Munich Communist government set up headquarters there, and in 1920 Hitler held his first meeting there with the National Socialists. The Nazi party used the hall to hold functions. Hitler proclaimed the twenty-five theses of the Nazi party at the Hofbräuhaus. After World War II, the Hofbräuhaus grew in international popularity. American soldiers stationed in Munich brought home clay mugs stamped with the Hofbräuhaus logo. The Hofbräuhaus has one of the largest tents at Oktoberfest and it is a very popular stopping point for people celebrating during the festival. Since the Hofbräuhaus has become more popular, other Hofbräuhauses have opened worldwide.

HOFBRÄUHAUS'S SOUR LUNG SOUP

Serves 4

1 tablespoon salt	4 tablespoon vinegar	0.4 liter red wine
1 tablespoon sugar	2 bunches of greens	1 tablespoon lemon juice
8 grains of pepper	2 leaves of laurel	2 onions
⅓ cup fat	1.7 liters water	500 grams veal lights (lungs)

Boil ingredients, add the cleaned lights, and let it cook for about one hour. Lift out lights, let them drip dry and cool down. Then cut them into fine strips, pour 0.5 liter of the broth and the vinegar over the strips and let it all marinate for one to two days. Take the listed ingredients and the broth and prepare a brown sauce, add the sliced lights, and season to taste. Serve with bread dumplings.

To make sauce, brown flour in butter, add onions, sauté onions, and add broth, a little at a time. Let cook, stirring constantly until sauce thickens.

Lederhosen are a good look for me, don't you think?

What to Wear

Lederhosen are known as the traditional costume in German-speaking countries, but they were historically worn as work garb because they are very durable, easy to work in, and easy to clean. *Lederhosen* translates to "leather pants" in German. Think of them as the great-great-grandpa to jeans. These days, lederhosen are for leisure and sometimes worn for traditional dinners or celebrations.

Yodeling

Yodeling is a form of singing in which the singer will sing one long note but change the pitch of the note rapidly. It's used in many cultures, but most well known for its role in Alpine folk music. The singing was originally used as a method of communication between alpine mountaineers and villagers. Yodeling helped voices carry over long distances. It turned into a traditional form of music in the Alpine area. Tahrir is a yodeling technique often used in Persian music. Try it for yourself: Yodel-Ay-EEE-Oooo.

Pucker Up

The brain detects a food's acidity through the taste buds. The more acidic a food is, the more sour it tastes. Something like a lemon, which has a large amount of citric acid, will really make your mouth pucker. In sour lung soup, the sour taste comes from vinegar in the sauce. The pH scale, which measures acid, runs from 0 to 14. Anything less than 7 is acidic and anything more than 7 is basic. Pure water is neutral and has a pH level of 7. Vinegar rates at 2.4, which explains why it tastes sour.

Why do sour foods make you pucker your lips? There has been no conclusion on why this happens, but it might be the body's reaction to stop you from eating bad foods. When milk goes bad, it has a sour taste. The body might pucker lips to prevent you from putting more in your mouth.

TASTES: BORN THIS WAY?

Scientists have done twin studies on fraternal and identical twins. Identical twins (who share the same DNA) have similar reactions to tasting foods, whereas fraternal twins (who have different DNA) have different reactions. This indicates that tastes may be genetic.

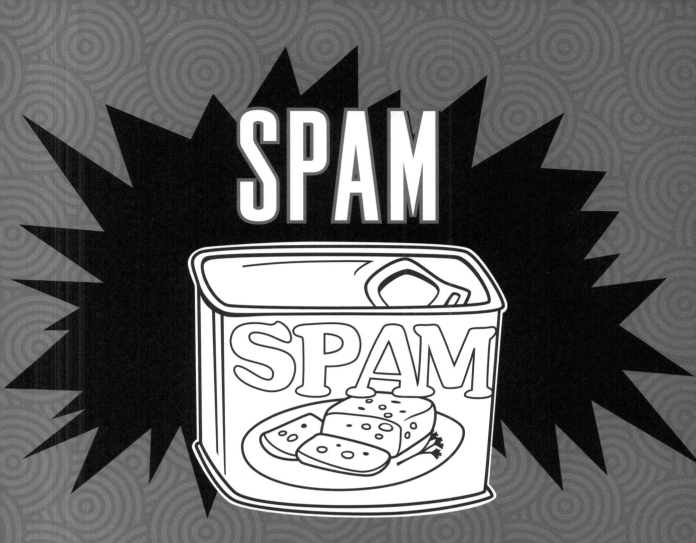

SPAM

Hormel Spiced Ham started as your average, basic, packaged meat product. However, sales were mediocre at best, and in 1936, the company offered a prize to the best new name for the canned meat. Kenneth Daigneau, an actor from New York, suggested the ingeniously simple name SPAM, melding the words "spiced" and "ham." Daigneau won $100, and the canned meat has been called SPAM ever since. (Interestingly, Kenneth's brother was Hormel VP Ralph Daigneau.)

The loaf of chopped pork shoulder, ham, modified potato starch, salt, water, and sodium nitrate (which keeps it fresh) is canned in SPAM's iconic blue packaging with yellow lettering. Since then, the world has consumed more than 7 billion cans of the stuff (and counting!). In 1998, the SPAM packaging was donated to the Smithsonian Institution.

During World War II, there was a meat shortage. Not only was it difficult to get protein to the soldiers, but it was also hard to find affordable meat at home. SPAM came to the rescue. The canned meat proved an inexpensive way to keep our boys overseas well nourished. It did not go bad quickly and the portions were easy to divvy up. It was affordable for families living at home. In 1943, Hormel took it a step further and launched a black-and-white economy label SPAM due to economic stress during the war. At the same time, SPAM was introduced to Guam, Hawaii, Saipan, and the Commonwealth of the Northern Mariana Islands, where it became a staple in the diet.

After the war ended, Hormel formed a group of ex-GIs, women known as the "Hormel Girls." They were sent across the United States to promote SPAM. The idea was to link eating SPAM to patriotism. In 1948, the group was made up of sixty women, sixteen of whom formed an orchestra. Their show became a radio show for quite some time. Some people believe SPAM was one reason the Allies were able to win the war.

In the United States, 3.8 cans of SPAM are eaten every second. Many Americans love SPAM, but no one loves it more than the people of Hawaii.

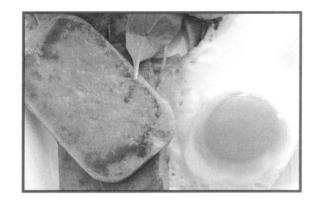

Hawaiians consume more SPAM per capita than anywhere else in the world, eating up to 4 million cans of SPAM every year. In Hawaii, SPAM is on the menu at McDonald's and Burger King.

I must confess: I loathe SPAM. What's to like? It's fake meat. I know some people are saying, "Andrew, SPAM isn't half as gross as some of the stuff you eat on the show." Sure, I eat the odd parts of animals all the time, but more times than not, it's very fresh meat. SPAM comes from weird, preservative-filled odds and ends. In my opinion, it's one of the egregious crimes against food nature. Scrapple and sisig (found in the Philippines), though similar to SPAM, are on a completely different level. Typically, they're homemade, created from real ingredients. The factory-made version is simply disgusting.

Am I grateful for SPAM? Of course; SPAM helped keep our troops fed during World War II. Will I be eating SPAM for lunch? Absolutely not.

SPAMTOWN, USA

Austin, Minnesota, the home of SPAM, is often called SPAMtown, USA. During the Independence Day festivities, the city celebrates with SPAM Jam, a festival dedicated to the food. Austin also houses the SPAM Museum, filled with 16,500 square feet of SPAM memorabilia, trivia, and even samples. Right across the street is Johnny's Main Event, a restaurant with Johnny's SPAMarama menu. Try anything from a SPAMburger to a SPAMpizza.

SPAM Museum in SPAMtown, USA.

SPAM Varieties

SPAM Classic not bizarre enough for you? Hormel makes a ton of different varieties of SPAM. Take your pick:

SPAM HICKORY SMOKED

SPAM WITH BACON

SPAM LITE

SPAM LESS SODIUM

SPAM SPREAD

SPAM WITH BLACK PEPPER

SPAM HOT & SPICY

SPAM WITH CHEESE

SPAM OVEN ROASTED TURKEY

And if you just can't choose:

SPAM VARIETY 12-PACK

Spamalot/Monty Python

Monty Python is a comedy group made up of six British comedians: Graham Chapman, John Cleese, Terry Gilliam, Eric Idle, Terry Jones, and Michael Palin. Monty Python grew popular in the late 1960s with their BBC sketch show called *Monty Python's Flying Circus*. The group went on to make books, music, and films.

One of Monty Python's most well-known sketches was called "SPAM." Two customers are at a café and want to order breakfast. They ask what's on the menu and the waitress lists each item, every one of them including SPAM. They manage to say "SPAM" more than one hundred times in a two-and-a-half-minute sketch. Bravo, I say. Bravo.

Eric Idle later created a Broadway musical called *Spamalot*, based on the Monty Python film, *Monty Python and the Holy Grail*. The name comes from a line in the film, "We eat ham, and jam, and SPAM a lot."

SPAM in the Inbox

The annoying e-mails that jam up your inbox have been dubbed "spam." The name comes from the afore-mentioned Monty Python sketch because "SPAM" is yelled an incredibly annoying amount of times. Spam can be any bulk and irritating e-mail from an adver-tisement, to someone trying to get personal informa-tion from you under a disguise as a "Nigerian prince" or "your distant relative," to a [No Subject] e-mail with a link to a virus.

FUN Facts

- Richard LeFevre holds the world record for eating SPAM by consuming a whopping 6 pounds in 12 minutes (see page 107).

- The Philippines is home to the SPAMJ Café, where most menu items contain SPAM, including SPAM Burgers, SPAM Club, SPAM Spaghetti, SPAM Nuggets, and SPAM Caesar Salad. Uff-da!

- SPAM is made in two U.S. locations: Austin, Minnesota, and Fremont, Nebraska. It is also made in seven countries abroad: Australia, Denmark, England, Japan, Philippines, South Korea, and Taiwan.

Spamasota!

Faith Farrell of "Nordeast" Minneapolis is an artist, meat raffle host, polka connoisseur, and award-winning hot-dish chef. In 2007, she dominated the National SPAM Recipe Cook-off with her Paul Bunyan–inspired Spamasota Hot-Dish recipe.

Faith Farrell shares her Spamasota hot-dish recipe with me. It's delicious, but so not good for the ol' waistline.

SPAMASOTA HOT-DISH (PAUL BUNYAN STYLE!)

Serves 6

- 1 can SPAM
- 1 bottle Summit Porter (or another porter beer)
- 2 tubes Pillsbury Grand butter biscuits
- 1 8-oz. container sour cream
- 6 oz. cream cheese
- About 1 cup half-and-half (needed to "cut" the thickness of the mixture)
- 1-2 tablespoons butter
- 1½ cups cheddar cheese
- ½ cup Parmesan cheese
- 2 cups wild rice
- 1 can cream of chicken soup
- 1 leek, sliced
- 1 bunch green onions, chopped
- 1 red pepper, diced (oooohhh— look! A vegetable! See? HEALTHY!)
- 2 turnips, cubed
- 1 teaspoon minced garlic
- crushed red pepper (to taste)
- ground black pepper
- 1 bag Old Dutch potato chips

- Rinse SPAM off and cut into cubes. Place cubes in bowl and soak with the porter beer from two hours to overnight.

- Read the directions on the Pillsbury Grand biscuits— cover bottom of your hot-dish pan with the biscuits and cook as directed. Let this cool.

- Get out the griddle, plop some butter in the pan—let the frying pan get hot—take the SPAM out from its yummy marinade, and brown the cubes in the butter.

- In lumberjack-sized bowl, mix in all the other ingredients except the potato chips. Be prepared for an upper-arm workout with all the heavy dairy and cheeses and turnips and SPAM doing their dance, dance revolution!!! (This is when the addition of the half-and-half works its magic—continue adding some half-and-half so mixture is more like stew and less like the consistency of concrete.)

- Once it is all mixed, place on top of the pre-cooked biscuits. Sprinkle with freshly ground pepper and some crushed red pepper flakes (per cook's personal taste—personally, I like a little ZING!).

- Rip open that bag of chips and crush the chips on top of this Big Foot–sized hot-dish!

- Bake at 350 degrees for an hour, until golden brown on top. The hot-dish is extra HOT, so make sure to let it stand for ten minutes so those flavors meld together!

- Enjoy in your home, the nearest pot luck, or any church basement. Raise your SPAM-ridden fork in a Swedish salute! SKOL! (That's a Scandinavian cheer for the rest of us!)

SQUID INK

Ever been so scared you've peed in your pants? Me neither, but I've been close. (Did you see the *Bizarre Foods* episode where I almost jumped off the nuclear reactor in South Africa . . . but chickened out? Yikes.) Squid, like most other cephalopods, have a similar problem. These animals have a mechanism that releases a blue-black ink when startled or threatened. The ink blocks sight and scent of the squid from its prey, allowing for the squid's swift getaway. The ink, a combination of melanin and mucus, is released through ink sacs located between the squid's gills. What's even odder to most people, stranger than a squid squirting ink out of its gills, is the fact that people eat the stuff. As an ingredient, the ink makes for fantastic flavoring and dramatic food coloring. Squid ink is most popular wherever it's freshest . . . like in the Mediterranean countries. It's used in stews, soups, pastas, and often served with the

squid itself. *Iron Chef America* fans will recall it was even used in ice cream.

Delicately briny and with just the faintest hint of lemons, the ink makes its best star turn in a quick braise over polenta or in a risotto. I can't get enough of the stuff.

The Pen

Today the ink used in pens is made from all sorts of pigments and dyes, but pen ink used to be made from cephalopod ink. Squid, octopus, and cuttlefish ink were all used to get varying colors. Cuttlefish release a brown-color ink. The color is now known as sepia, which is the Greek word for "cuttlefish."

Pasta colored with squid ink.

HOW TO ▶ Harvest Squid Ink

GET A SQUID. Go fishing or buy one at a store. (Make sure the squid has not been "pre-cleaned"; if it has, the ink is gone.)

REMOVE THE INK SAC by detaching the squid head from its body. The internal organs will come along with the head. See the silvery sac in the middle of the organs? That's the ink sac. Cut out the ink sac from either side.

COLLECT THE INK. Get a bowl (that you don't mind if it turns black), fill with 1 tablespoon of water, put the sac in the bowl, and puncture it with a knife.

ENJOY. Use it as a delicious ingredient!

Squid on a stick.

SQUID

There are 300 different species of squid, all with eight arms and two long tentacles. They all also have a mantle, which is flesh that covers their main body. However, you'll see huge differences in their size. The smallest squids can be less than as 1 inch long. The largest can be up to 45 feet long.

Compared to their body sizes, squids have large eyes and they have excellent eyesight. To move, squids use a siphon—a small, narrow tube. They can suck in water and push water out of the siphon to propel themselves forward.

ARM VS. TENTACLE

A squid has eight arms and two tentacles. So what's the difference, right? An arm has tiny suction cups all the way down it. Tentacles are longer than arms and only have the suction cups at the end of the appendages.

THE COLOSSAL SQUID

Sailors used to fear the Kraken, a giant sea monster that would take down ships with its large tentacles. No proof of a Kraken has ever been found, but it could be very possible that sailors were spotting colossal squids and giant squids. These elusive animals live 3,000 feet under the sea, and their existence is only known because they've been accidentally caught in fishermen's nets or found in the bellies of whales. They've never been seen in their natural habitat, though giant squids have been captured on camera.

Colossal and giant squids reach enormous sizes due to abyssal gigantism. This is a phenomena that states that deep-sea animals tend to be much larger than their "not-deep-sea" counterparts. There are a couple of theories on why this happens. One is that there is less food in the deep, so the creatures must be a giant size to travel long distances for food. Another is called Bergmann's Rule. Bergmann's Rule states that animals will be smaller in hot environments and larger in cold environments. Since there is no sunlight in the deep sea, it is very cold. Bergmann's Rule explains that animals in cold environments need to create more body heat to keep warm, whereas animals in hot environments need to create as little body heat as possible.

The colossal squid is more massive than the giant squid. It's the largest known invertebrate on earth. They also hold the title for the largest eyes on the planet—up to 10 inches in diameter, about the size of a basketball. The eyes take in 144 times as much light as the human eye. This is most likely because it is so dark where they live.

OTHER GIANT SEA CREATURES

BATHYNOMUS GIGANTEUS

Commonly known as the giant isopod, these deep Atlantic scavengers gorge themselves on dead whales, fish, and squid until they're so full, they can barely move. Weighing in at almost 4 pounds, they look like enormous bugs, and in fact, they sort of are. Some of their closest relatives are wood lice—not to be confused with head lice, which is a completely different thing altogether.

JAPANESE SPIDER CRAB

The leggiest of the arthropod family, this marine crab measures 12 feet long from claw to claw. As the name suggests, it's found mostly off the coast of Japan and can be eaten. Fishermen, be warned . . . these strong crabs can pack quite a pinch.

GIANT OARFISH

Found in the world's tropical oceans, the King of Herrings is listed in the *Guinness World Records* as the planet's largest bony fish. These puppies can reach over 56 feet in length, making them about 16 feet longer than a school bus. Despite their large size, these fish typically feed on zooplankton and tiny crustaceans . . . and are a favorite food of sharks.

Japanese spider crab—handle with care!

A Different Kind of Ink: Chef Tattoos

Chefs are right up there with rock stars and bikers in their love for ink. No, not the kind from a squid—the kind you get at a tattoo parlor. Here are some of my fave food tatts:

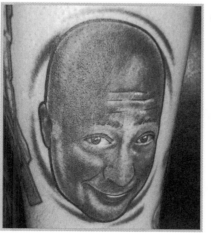

As far as I'm concerned, tattoo artist Ben Hatfield is my number-one fan. Can you top this?

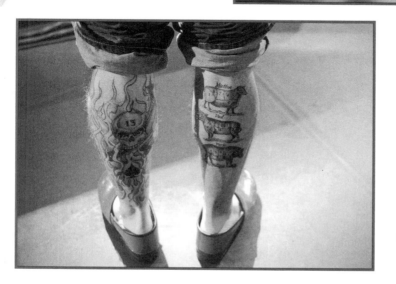

My buddy Michael Symon: Iron Chef, pork lover, fellow baldie.

Chef Rick Tramonto rocks the salty, the sweet *(awww!)*, and the seafood.

stuffed Lamb spleen

The spleen is a multipurpose organ. It removes old blood cells. It recycles iron. Since one of the spleen's main jobs is to store extra blood, spleen has a very strong iron and mineral flavor. In a butcher shop, spleen often goes under the name "melt." It is very inexpensive and is seldom eaten in the United States. You're more likely to find spleen in the pet-food aisle than you are in the deli. So, consider the case of Fido's mystery meat solved.

But just 'cause spleen is a common dog-food ingredient doesn't mean you ought to scoff at it. This stuff is delicious in sausages. It can be grilled or roasted, braised, and (my favorite way to eat spleen) stuffed with garlic, tomatoes, fatty cuts of other meats, and spices. It's much better than a can of dog food. In the Middle East and North Africa it is served hot or cold, but here is the rub: Because there is so little intra-muscular fat in a spleen, not only is it massively

organ-y in flavor, but it's very tough and mealy in texture. If you don't like your spleen stuffed, try a braised spleen sandwich in Sardinia. It might be more your style. Lamb spleen is tastier than cow spleen, in case you were wondering.

Stuffed lamb spleen, served right off the grill in Morocco.

your spleen

The spleen is a hard worker. It has multiple jobs: storing blood, clearing out foreign bodies and old blood cells, and recycling iron in the blood. As part of the lymphatic system, it works to keep bodily fluid levels in balance and defend the body against infections. The human spleen is about the size of a fist. It's not a vital organ, but people who have their spleens removed lose part of their immune system and tend to get more bacterial infections. Before modern science, people believed the spleen harbored evil intentions. So, when someone would express their anger, it was called "venting their spleen." The spleen is a very bright red. Some butchers will put spleen in their ground beef to pump up the red coloring.

LAMB VS. MUTTON

Male sheep are rams, female sheep are ewes, and baby sheep are lambs. They are lambs up until about a year of age. So when you order lamb off the menu, it is a young sheep. The older sheep is called mutton. Sheep are not only raised for meat but also for their milk and fleece. Flocks of sheep tend to stay close together, chowing down on grass or short plants they can find. Interestingly, most sheep are born as twins.

ORGANS YOU CAN LIVE WITHOUT

If needed, your body could function without a spleen. Other organs you can function without?

APPENDIX The vermiform appendix hangs off the end of the colon. It looks like a worm, which is where the term "vermiform" comes from—it means "wormlike." In the modern human, the appendix has no functional purpose. The theory is the appendix once had a purpose, possibly to catch bones and other indigestible things humans might have consumed. Things can still get caught in the appendix during digestion, causing inflammation. This is called appendicitis and requires the removal of the appendix.

GALLBLADDER The gallbladder has a few functions. It helps digest fat and will concentrate bile produced by the liver. When the gallbladder is removed, there is no place for the bile to be stored. The liver will still produce the same amount of bile, you just won't have as much in your intestine without the storage space.

ONE LUNG For most of us, as we breathe in, our two lungs fill with oxygen. This is the most efficient way to breathe, but it is possible to live with only one lung, though with half of the lung power, breathing is more difficult.

ONE KIDNEY Kidneys have several functions, including filtering blood and removing waste to the urinary bladder. Most people are born with two, but if one has to be removed, your body can fully function with one. You may voluntarily give up one kidney and donate it to someone who needs one.

TONSILS The tonsils are the big lumps on either side of the back of your throat. They are part of the lymphatic system and are believed to defend against upper respiratory infections. If you come down with strep throat one too many times, the most common defensive action is to have the tonsils removed. It seems counterintuitive but can help a lot.

SOME PARTS OF THE BRAIN The brain is a tricky organ to live without. As long as the parts of the brain remain that control breathing, swallowing, and all of the necessary functions to live, you can stay alive with some missing parts. But removing portions of the brain also may remove your capability of carrying out other functions like speaking, understanding speech, seeing, etc.

PARTS OF THE INTESTINES The intestines are necessary for proper digestion, but since they are so long, not all of the intestines are necessary to live. Since there is less storage for waste, removing parts of the intestines will increase the amount of times you would have to go to the bathroom . . . and decrease the amount of time you have to get there.

COUNTING SHEEP

Have you ever tried counting sheep to fall asleep? The idea is that watching one fluffy sheep after another jump over a fence will bore you to sleep. According to studies done by Oxford University, counting sheep does not really induce sleep. Researchers recommend imagining a beach or a waterfall instead, which exudes more mental energy and will help you fall asleep faster.

DOLLY

On July 5, 1996, a lamb was born. Her name was Dolly. Dolly wasn't just any regular little lamb; her birth was historical. Dolly was the first cloned mammal. She had three different mothers: One provided the DNA, the second provided an egg that the DNA was injected into, and the third carried Dolly. The scientists at Roslin Institute in Scotland tried 276 attempts before Dolly's birth was possible.

THE WOOL TRUTH...

Wool is an amazing fiber and it all comes from sheep's fur, which is called fleece. Sheep farmers will shear their sheep when their coats get long. They will collect the fleece and scour, or clean, it. The fleece is then spun into a yarn, which can be made into clothes, blankets, toys, and a plethora of other things. One pound of wool can make 10 miles of yarn. Wool is an extremely tough fiber. It's comparatively stronger than steel and it's fire resistant, according to the American Sheep Industry Association.

tarantulas

Of all the foods I have eaten in my lifetime, the tarantula strikes me as one of the strangest from a psychological standpoint. We are pre-conditioned in this country to think of these fuzzy insects as scary and poisonous, belonging on Halloween decorations, not dinner plates. But they taste great, reminding me of land crabs, sweet and delicate. I only eat them fresh; I have gotten pretty picky. I need to see them go from basket to wok to me. I don't eat pre-bunned hot dogs on the street and I don't eat pre-cooked tarantulas. Couple of reasons: Freshness counts and even in many Southeast Asian countries where tarantulas are commonly eaten, some vendors hawk less-than-fresh product. The flavor of an old fried tarantula is unpleasant, reeking of fryer oil and lacking all the sugary nuance of a fresh crab. And second, once you've defanged your own tarantulas in Skuon and eaten them hot from the wok, you never go back to street spiders. Traveling and eating can spoil a man.

Sometimes necessity drives culinary trends. The Khmer Rouge—a political party that ruled Cambodia in the 1970s—set out to make the country an agrarian-based Communist society. The party's policies led to severe poverty, famine, and death. Hungry Cambodians looked to alternative proteins, and many people began eating tarantulas and other insects. More than thirty years later, Cambodians still enjoy this eight-legged snack.

Few regions enjoy eating "a-ping" (the local lingo for tarantulas) more than the people of Skuon, Cambodia. The process of harvesting and preparing the delicacy is an arduous one, which begins with expert spider hunters luring the furry arachnids out of deep burrows with sticks. The skilled (and brave) hunters pluck the fangs from a spider's mouth, rendering the venomous arachnid defenseless. It's a good thing—although a tarantula bite is no more poisonous than a bee string, they hurt like heck.

Crickets and tarantulas for sale in Cambodia. Chow down!

Covered with Cambodian tarantulas—
just another day at the office.

The defanged spiders are then sold to spider mongers who prepare them for consumption. Since the arachnids live in underground holes, they must first be rinsed of dirt. They're then tossed in a mixture of spices—usually salt, garlic, and sugar—then fried in a big, oil-filled wok. If you happen to assist in a tarantula chef's kitchen, keep a good distance from the wok. The frying carcasses may explode! The spiders must sizzle for at least three minutes, long enough to singe all the hairs from their body, which irritate the throat and can numb the tongue.

Most fried spiders sell for about 25 cents apiece, and spider hawkers can make up to $25 a day—a huge sum given that of one-third the Cambodian population makes $1 or less per day. The palm-sized tarantulas are eaten whole—legs, abdomen, head, and all. Those who visit Cambodia in winter may get an extra-special treat. December is tarantula baby-making time, and half of the spiders are bursting with eggs.

So what do these giant, hairy spiders taste like? Not bad—comparable to a soft-shell crab (not surprising since they're both arthropods), sweet, nutty, and downright delicious. Though the egg sacks have a meaty texture, they're mostly flavorless. For the best eating, stick to the face.

Fun Facts about Tarantulas

- Tarantulas are carnivores and love a meal of insects, frogs, toads, and mice. The giant spider grabs its prey with its legs, then injects its victim with a paralyzing, poisonous venom. It secretes digestive enzymes that liquefy its victims' bodies. The tarantula will suck them up like a strawberry milk shake through its strawlike mouth openings. After a large meal, the stuffed tarantula may not need to eat for a month.

- Thinking about keeping a tarantula as a pet? Keep in mind that these hairy creatures can live up to thirty years. Most pet tarantulas survive on a diet solely of gut-loaded crickets (meaning crickets that have recently eaten). It's common for larger tarantulas to dine on about six crickets per week. Over thirty years, that adds up to more than 9,300 crickets.

This guy found good eatin'—a cockroach!

- Nice legs! An average tarantula will grow to about 4.75 inches long with a leg span of up to 11 inches. A full-grown tarantula weighs in at about 1–3 ounces.

- Periodically, tarantulas shed their exoskeletons. They can also replace some internal organs and will regenerate lost appendages.

- While you sleep, spiders hunt. But no need to fret over that old wives' tale that claims people swallow more than eight spiders in their sleep each year—it's a myth. Though these nocturnal creatures do love crawling into dark cavernous structures, your breathing is enough to keep most spiders out. Your ears on the other hand . . .

- Planning on gussying up for a special occasion? Try dining on tarantulas. Many Cambodian women believe eating these hairy spiders makes one beautiful. Or you could just slap on a little lipstick.

- Got something in your teeth? Tarantula fangs are used as toothpicks by the Piaroa Indians of Venezuela.

Phobias

The Mayo Clinic (not to be confused with the Mayonnaise Clinic) defines a phobia as "an overwhelming and unreasonable fear of an object or situation that poses little real danger." You've probably heard of one of the most common phobias: arachnophobia, or fear of spiders. However, there are lots of much weirder phobias out there. See if you can match the official phobia name with its definition.

1. **Bald people**

2. **Chopsticks**

3. **Creepy, crawly things**

4. **Eating or swallowing, or being eaten**

5. **Flutes**

6. **Garlic**

7. **Peanut butter sticking to the roof of the mouth**

8. **Phobias**

9. **School**

10. **Teenagers**

11. **Vomiting**

12. **Words, long**

A. Ephebiphobia

B. Scolionophobia

C. Alliumphobia

D. Consecotaleophobia

E. Arachibutyrophobia

F. Hippopotomonstroses-quippedaliophobia

G. Aulophobia

H. Emetophobia

I. Peladophobia

J. Phagophobia

K. Herpetophobia

L. Phobophobia

(Answers: 1I, 2D, 3K, 4J, 5G, 6C, 7E, 8L, 9B, 10A, 11H, 12F)

TONGUE

Tongue has been a beloved food since the Stone Age—for real. The thick muscle that sits in the mouth appealed to Paleolithic hunters who craved hearty, bone-sticking meals. Eons later, we're still enjoying tongue. It's a favorite food in places like Poland, Mexico, Italy, China, France . . . well, everywhere really. And it's making a big comeback here in our country after being a second-class citizen for about a generation and a half.

Tongue's characteristics make it a very special meat. It's boneless, it has more protein than a steak and half the fat, and it comes in as many varieties as there are travelers on Noah's Ark . . . beef, pork, lamb, and even duck! Tongue can be prepared any way you like it. The Belgians prefer their tongue with mushroom sauce. Some enjoy it pickled, then cooked, or smoked. In France, duck tongues are served deep-fried. Any way you eat it, tongue will keep your taste buds happy (no pun intended). Properly cooked, it has a supremely meaty flavor that is very intense. Cow's tongue, for example, tastes like short ribs but has the texture of perfectly crafted pot roast.

It's better than Christmas (sorry, Santa, no offense).

How does this delicacy go from a lump of muscles to a delightful dish? The tongue should first be soaked in cold water for several hours. This cleans and softens the meat. Next, trim the visibly extraneous cartilage and fat from the tongue. Throw a cow tongue in a pot of salted water seasoned with plenty of chopped celery and onion, and let it simmer a few hours. Once cooked, take the tongue out. Peel it. Trim again. Eat it. I like mine on rye toast with spicy pickled onions and a schmear of brown mustard.

Tongue on rye, a deli treat.

Taste Buds

Taste buds are your best buds. They let you enjoy all of the wonderful foods you stick in your mouth by detecting any sweet, sour, salty, and bitter flavors. They're made up of taste cells, which have tiny microscopic hairs called microvilli that send all of the flavor info to the brain. Humans are born with 10,000 taste buds, but as we age the taste buds die and a person can have as few as 5,000 taste buds. That is why some foods taste stronger to children than to adults. Taste buds can also be inhibited by cold temperatures. So, here is a tip: If you have to eat a food you know you don't like, put an ice cube on your tongue first. It will dull the flavor.

Tongue (Yours)

- You've probably heard it before: "The tongue is the strongest muscle in the body." It's partially true. The tongue is very strong, but it is actually not a single muscle. It's made up of eight.

- The average length of a human tongue is 4 inches.

- Every human has a unique "tongue print," like your fingerprints.

- The frenulum is the thin layer of tissue that connects your tongue to the bottom of your mouth.

- The top of the tongue is covered with tiny bumps called papillae. They grip food and move it while you chew. They also have taste buds in them.

- The tongue never sleeps. The tongue is constantly working—eating, talking, tasting, etc. Even when we sleep, the tongue pushes saliva to the back of the throat, so you don't drool all over the pillow.

Animal Tongues

Tongues are often taken for granted. They help us to eat, swallow, and not drool all over ourselves. Some animal tongues have even more uses:

- Cats use their tongues to clean their fur. Their rough tongues are able to remove oils and parasites.

- A dog's tongue acts as a heat regulator. When a dog exercises, the blood flow to its tongue increases. The dog will stick its tongue out, and the cool air will decrease the blood flow to the tongue along with the dog's body heat. That is why a dog pants when it runs or if it's hot outside.

- Cattle move their tongues 40,000 to 60,000 times per day just by chewing, and their tongues can weigh up to 5 pounds. That's a well-exercised muscle—which is why it's so beautifully dense and marbled, perfect for slow cooking and eating.

- Giraffes' tongues are blackish-blue in color. They can be 14 to 20 inches long. They're so long that giraffes use their tongues to clean their ears, which is pretty disgusting.

- A snake has an organ on the roof of its mouth called the Jacobson's organ, which acts as a chemical receptor. A snake will flick out its tongue and put the ends into the organ. The organ sends messages to the snake's brain letting it know what chemicals are in the air. It can sense fear, danger, and its proximity to the nearest Old Country Buffet. Okay, one of those was just speculation.

- The alligator snapping turtle has a red appendage at the end of its tongue that looks like a worm. It uses the worm to lure prey into its mouth.

- Some animals have prehensile tongues, which means their tongues can grasp or hold objects, like a monkey's tail. These include frogs and anteaters, and animals that catch their prey with their tongues.

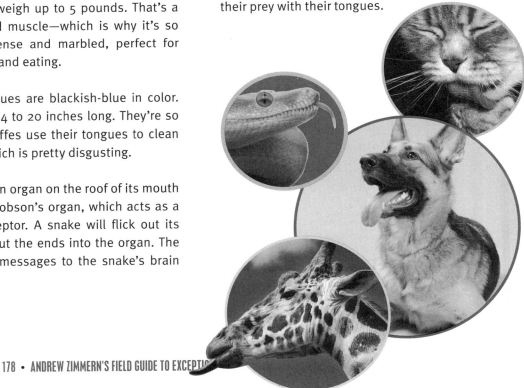

Tongue Sayings

Have you ever tried to say something, but it just didn't come out right? That's called being tongue-tied. It would be hard to talk with your tongue tied in a knot. Here are some tongue phrases that are good to know.

TONGUE-TIED: Means not being able to say what you want. It is also a medical condition called ankyloglossia, where the frenulum is located too close to the tip of the tongue and limits the tongue's movement.

CAT GOT YOUR TONGUE?: Unknown origins. Most likely, it comes from the British Navy where sailors were punished by being whipped with a cat-o'-nine-tails. The sailors were in so much pain they were unable to speak afterward, thus "cat got your tongue?"

TIP OF THE TONGUE: When people say, "it's on the tip of my tongue," it means they are unable to retrieve a word or name. This is an actual phenomenon where the brain is unable to recall information that it knows it possesses.

TONGUE IN CHEEK: This saying means a statement was made ironically or should not be taken at face value. Historically, it was a sign of contempt to "put one's tongue into cheek."

Mind Your Manners

In the United States and some other parts in the world, it is considered rude to stick out your tongue. It's even worse if you blow a raspberry (aka make a fart noise). In Rome, it's actually against the law to stick out your tongue at someone, and offenders may face big fines. However, in some places like Tibet, it is completely polite to stick out your tongue. It's a way of saying hello in a respectful manner. Best rule of thumb: Keep your tongue to yourself if you don't know the cultural rules.

TONGUE TWISTERS

THE SIXTH SICK SHEIK'S SIXTH SHEEP'S SICK

IRISH WRISTWATCH

SHINY SUSHI

TURDUCKEN

Sitting at the local Poultry A-Go-Go and fraught with worry over what to order? Order the turducken and get the best of everything. This ingenious dish is a boneless chicken stuffed inside a boneless duck, stuffed inside a boneless turkey . . . then roasted. In the United Kingdom, it goes by the Dickensian moniker of the "three-bird roast" or "royal roast." Here in the States, we just squish all the words together to make one super-sized gibberish word: turduck-en. Ugh. And frankly the made-up nature of the word itself is a marketing problem. Childish

names deserve childish consideration. Now, a "royal roast" sounds like something you'd want to try, doesn't it? You should, it's delicious!

"Nesting," the technique of cooking foods stuffed inside other foods, dates back to the golden days of stuffing. That would be the seventeenth century, but the franken-bird wasn't produced commercially until 1985 when Hebert's Specialty Meats (HSM) in Maurice, Louisiana, started making them for local customers. NFL analyst John Madden raved about the stuffed birds during a Thanksgiving game and presented

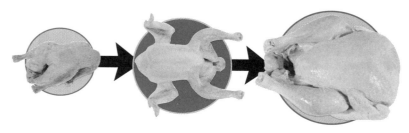

the winning team with turducken after the contest. This pushed the sales for turducken into the national consciousness, and today, Sam Hebert and his family-run butcher shop produce and ship nearly 5,000 turduckens around Thanksgiving alone. And there are hundreds of companies around the country doing the same thing. The nice thing about HSM is that they will stuff your turducken with any one of a dozen types of sausage and force-meat—or stuff just about anything inside anything else. No jokes, please.

You should visit HSM, buy some turducken, ship it home, and then have lunch at the café next door run by Sam's eight sisters. The gumbo is without peer.

If you're hankering for turducken, there's no better place than Hebert's in Louisiana.

Great Nesting Meals

Turducken-like meals date all the way back to the ancient Romans, who would make "nested" meals for their royalty.

- According to the BBC, in December 2007, a family living on a farm in Devon, England, created a roast consisting of twelve "nested" birds. The birds included turkey, goose, chicken, pheasant, three ducks, poussin, guinea fowl, partridge, pigeon squab, and quail. The meal weighed 55 pounds and took two people to lift. After roasting for ten hours, it could feed up to 125 people.

- Whole stuffed camel: A traditional Bedouin wedding dish, this consists of a camel stuffed with a sheep, stuffed with chicken, stuffed with fish, stuffed with cooked eggs.

- Merrick Pet Care sells turducken cat food.

- Why didn't we think of this earlier? Turducken covered in bacon. The turbaconducken.

portmanteau

The word "turducken" is a combination of three words: turkey, duck, and chicken. Combining words to make a word is called a portmanteau. Here are a few others you might be familiar with:

SPANISH + **ENGLISH** = **SPANGLISH**

BREAKFAST + **LUNCH** = **BRUNCH**

MOTOR + **HOTEL** = **MOTEL**

SMOKE + **FOG** = **SMOG**

TANGANYIKA + **ZANZIBAR** = **TANZANIA**

INFORMATION + **COMMERCIAL** = **INFOMERCIAL**

Make your own portmanteaus! It's easy—just take a word and add another. For example, an ugly meal that tastes delicious is uglicious.

HOW TO MAKE A TURDUCKEN

1. Get your hands on a turkey, a chicken, and a duck.

2. Cut the birds down the middle on the backbone side so the meat can lay flat.

3. Rinse the birds.

4. Debone the birds.

5. Layer turkey, stuffing, duck, stuffing, chicken, stuffing.

6. Close the turducken with skewers or twine.

7. Roast the turducken and enjoy!

TWINKIES

Twinkies and I go way back. Hate to admit it, but I am the Twinkie Generation—born into a Twinkie world, not knowing any better until years later. Twinkies are like a crazy ex-girlfriend. She looked great when I met her, and I suffered no ill effects early on in the relationship, but years into it, all my friends said she might kill me. Twinkies are like that.

First off there is the positive side. We all need to have our guilty pleasures, so the occasional Twinkie or four or five, with a glass of milk, is not a bad idea . . . for me. But regular consumption of a product so closely related to plastic on the molecular level is hard to swallow as a parent. Literally. This snack cake is way too sugary to even allow my kid to try one. Does not letting him taste a Twinkie make me a bad dad or father of the year?

I eat two Twinkies a year. One deep-fried and sugar-dipped at the Minnesota State Fair and one on a road trip with coffee. But only when no one is looking.

EVERLASTING TWINKIES?

Prepackaged baked goods line the shelves of supermarkets. From Zebra Cakes and Ho Hos to Nutty Bars and Sno Balls, kids scream for snack cakes. However, no cellophane-wrapped sugar buzz garners more attention than the infamous Twinkie. The rumor mill churns with supposed Twinkie facts—notably, that they last forever, can survive a nuclear attack, and that the top secret Twinkie-riffic ingredient is embalming fluid.

Not the case. First of all, the embalming fluid thing is just an urban (and suburban) myth. And while Twinkies were a common staple in many a 1960s bomb shelter, they can't survive a nuclear attack. In fact, Hostess claims a Twinkie's shelf life is only twenty-six days—far longer than most bakery items, but a blip in time when compared to eternity.

So that demystifies the everlasting Twinkie myth . . . or does it? Retired Maine science teacher Roger Bennatti decided to find out for himself. "We were discussing food chemistry and preservatives, and a student asked how long a Twinkie would last," explains Bennatti. "I said, 'I don't know. Let's do an experiment.' I sent a student to the grocery store next to the school to buy a package of Twinkies. I unwrapped the package, ate one, and placed the second atop the chalkboard."

Nearly thirty-five years later, the snack cake is dusty and hardened with a few specks of mold—but still looks a whole lot like a Twinkie. How long does he think a Twinkie will last? "Perhaps twenty-six days if you want to eat it," says Bennatti. "Forever, if you just want to stare at it."

THE TWINKIE DEFENSE . . . FACT OR FICTION?

Defendant Dan White claimed intense depression pushed him to murder both San Francisco city supervisor Harvey Milk and mayor George Moscone in 1979. As evidence of his altered mental state, his legal team cited White's junk food diet, including a supposed binge on Twinkies the night before the murders. This sugar-buzz explanation for murder made big waves in the headlines, and the "Twinkie Defense" was born.

But here's where things get sticky. White's legal team claims Twinkies were barely mentioned in court, and jurors said this sugar argument played little into their final verdict. It's said that San Francisco–based satirist Paul Krassner coined the phrase the "Twinkie Defense," and it just sort of stuck. Whether or not Twinkies actually played a role in the jury sentencing White (he was charged with voluntary manslaughter), the phrase is still used as legal slang for an improbable legal defense.

Cream-Filled Snacks Facts

- Twinkies are 4 inches long by 1½ inches wide.

- Of the Twinkies' thirty-nine ingredients, eight are derived from corn.

- Five hundred million Twinkies are sold every year.

- Invented by vice president for Continental Baking Company James "Jimmy" A. Dewar in Schiller Park (1930). He created the recipe to utilize machines that made cream-filled strawberry shortcake. The machines were not used when strawberries were out of season.

- While Dewar was driving to St. Louis to show off his new creation, he saw a billboard for Twinkle Toe Shoes, and he came up with the name "Twinkies."

- The original Twinkies were filled with banana cream, but bananas were rationed during World War II and Hostess switched to a vanilla cream and kept the flavor due to popularity.

- President Bill Clinton put a Twinkie in the U.S. government's millennium time capsule.

- Twinkies are approximately 68 percent air.

- New Orleans consumes more Twinkies per year compared to other U.S. cities.

- The original recipe used basic ingredients like eggs, milk, and butter. Its two-day shelf life made stocking the snack expensive— eventually chemical ingredients were added to increase the shelf life.

Five Ways to Eat a Twinkie

1. Frozen
2. Twinkie Kabobs (cut Twinkie into cubes, skewer with fruit)
3. Deep-fried
4. As sushi (see page 186)
5. Twinkie Wiener Sandwich (cut the Twinkie down the middle, put a hot dog on it)

"TWINKIES WAS THE BEST DARN-TOOTIN' IDEA I EVER HAD."
—Jimmy Dewar,
inventor of the Twinkie

"WANT A TWINKIE, GENGHIS KHAN?"
—Ted, *Bill and Ted's Excellent Adventure*

TWINKIE SUSHI

3 Hostess Twinkies
Assorted dried fruits
Assorted fruity candies
  (Swedish Fish are perfect)
2 green fruit roll-ups
Dried mangoes (looks like pickled ginger)

For sushi rolls: Cut one Twinkie into four to six pieces, depending on how large you want the sushi to be. Wrap each piece with slices of the Fruit Roll-Ups (see photo). Lay each piece flat and adorn with gummy candy and/ or dried fruit.

For sushi pieces: Wrap slices of the Fruit Roll-Up around a piece of Twinkie and a gummy fish. Delish!

FUN WITH SCIENCE!

What do you get when you mix two college dudes, finals week, and a box of Twinkies? Tests With Inorganic Noxious Kakes in Extreme Situations aka "T.W.I.N.K.I.E.S."—a series of scientific experiments performed by Rice University students Todd Stadler and Chris Gouge in 1995.

"Our 'project' was decidedly not for class," says Stadler. "It was a way to procrastinate instead of studying for finals in my sophomore (Chris's freshman) year. Basically, the idea was, 'Hey, let's do stupid "scientific" experiments on Twinkies and put it up on our Web page!' Not the highest of concepts. But at least it wasn't studying."

The duo performed seven time-sucking experiments in total, including a Gravitational Response Test (aka dropping a Twinkie off the sixth floor of a building), and Radiation Response Test (microwaving the Twinkie for ten minutes). Let's just say the radiation test is not recommended— just over one minute in, they abandoned ship due to "noxious fumes" and "copious amounts of smoke."

"The scientific value of what we did is highly suspect," says Stadler. "The whole project is really more a mockery of the scientific process (as some people understand it) than actual science. That hasn't stopped a large number of teachers from contacting me to say they use the Web site to teach kids about science. I'm ambivalent about this accomplishment in the field of education."

A HAIKU

MICROWAVED TWINKIES EMIT A GREAT DEAL OF SMOKE AND SMELL VERY BAD

—Todd Stadler

Wildebeest

You've undoubtedly seen this nature video: a herd of wildebeests hanging out along the banks of the Nile River, cooling off and hydrating. All of a sudden, an enormous crocodile pounces, ferociously biting one of the wildebeests on the neck. It's croc dinnertime. Not only are wildebeests a hungry crocodile's ideal meal, but cheetahs, lions, wild dogs, and hyenas love them just as much. Oh, and we like them too. Africa is home to vast herds of wildebeests, and it's no surprise that they're commonly eaten across the southern half of the continent. With a robust beefy texture and distinctly mild flavor, wildebeest is farmed for its meat but is also beautifully tender when taken in the wild. Like other African antelope such as kudu, springbok, oryx, and gazelle, the wildebeest has some of the best-tasting meat in the animal kingdom.

When I was in Namibia, I shot a blue wildebeest that was nearly 700 pounds from a distance

A blue wildebeest I shot in Namibia. It took me over three hours to clean, and yes, I did it myself!

of about 150 yards. We field-dressed the animal, ate some of the meat for lunch, and donated the rest to a tribal guide's family who was mourning the death of a loved one, as well as to a small boarding school that hadn't seen meat in months. The skin and skull are in my office, and so is the scrotum that I use as a small pouch for keeping my cuff links. I know . . . I am a dork.

Wildebeest Fun Facts

"Wildebeest" translates to "wild beast" or "wild cattle" in Dutch. Although they look like cattle, wildebeests are actually a type of antelope. Other facts you might not know about these creatures:

- Wildebeests just won't shut up. These noisy animals make a variety of loud noises, ranging from quick snorts to weird moans. That's why many African tribes call wildebeests "gnus" after the noise they make.

- Wildebeests stick together. Aside from humans, they live in more densely packed groups than any other mammal.

- There are two species of wildebeest: the blue wildebeest that has a silvery blue sheen to its hide, and the black wildebeest that is almost extinct in the wild. The black wildebeests that are surviving today live in captivity in zoos and on game farms.

- Wildebeests live an average of twenty years and reach 8 feet in length and can be 4.5 feet tall. They typically weigh around 600 pounds.

- Wildebeests are often shown on wildlife documentaries as a stampeding animal. They actually have a defense mechanism known as "swarm intelligence," where they spread out and move as one group. This creates a larger obstacle for their predators to combat with.

- Wildebeests have a large head and shaggy mane. Both male and female wildebeests grow horns.

MORE Wildebeest FUN Facts!

- Wildebeests live in places with grassy plains and open woodlands in central, southern, and eastern Africa, where they graze on grass. It's also important for wildebeests to live near water sources since they need to drink water every day.

- Every year, 500,000 calves are born in February and March, and they can walk within minutes of being born. Female wildebeests all tend to give birth around the same time.

- If a baby wildebeest loses its mother, it will imprint on what it sees next—whether it be a person, another animal, a Jeep, or even a predator (oops).

- Wildebeests can run up to 40 miles per hour, and will reach that speed faster than you can say *hakuna matata*.

- Wildebeests have scent glands on their hooves that they use to mark their territories.

MIGRATION

When animals move great distances for a new habitat annually or seasonally, it's called a migration. Wildebeests take part in one of the largest migrations on Earth, covering nearly 2,000 miles round-trip. Every year, about 1.5 million wildebeests travel from the Serengeti, where they spend most of February grazing and birthing their calves, to the Masai Mara of Kenya, where the rainy season is just beginning. From March until May, the herd migrates in the direction of the rain.

Although the wildebeest migration is the largest in the world, other animals move in mass as well. Here are a few:

MONARCH BUTTERFLY:

Every winter, millions of monarch butterflies migrate from parts of North America to specific forests in Southern California and Mexico—the same exact forest its ancestors have visited for generations. What's especially odd is that a butterfly's life span maxes out at eight months, meaning the butterflies complete the up-to-3,000-mile migration having never been to the destination before. It's thought that the butterflies are born with a sort of biological GPS system that keeps them on track.

ATLANTIC SALMON:

Atlantic salmon follow an anadromous fish migration pattern—they move from fresh water to salt water and back. They're born in fresh water, where they grow stronger and larger. As they reach adulthood, they migrate to salt water. They will live their adult life in salt water until it comes time to spawn, in which they will return to the fresh water to lay and fertilize their eggs. All Pacific salmon die after spawning; about 90 percent of Atlantic salmon will die as well. The cycle begins again when the eggs hatch, releasing newly born salmon.

BIRDS:

Many species of birds migrate during the switch from winter to summer. Similar to the monarch butterflies, they will use an internal sun compass to know where they are going. The birds are most often flying to somewhere with more food and better weather conditions. It's also suspected they are big fans of the smothered-'n'-covered hash browns at Waffle House.

SNOWBIRDS:

As adult humans begin retiring, they often migrate to southern states, particularly Florida and Arizona, where they will set up residence during the winter months. These snowbirds will often be spotted by the pool, playing shuffleboard, walking around the block, and/or golfing. Males can't seem to get enough of Tommy Bahama silk shirts, or white sneakers with black socks. Females prefer matching sleeveless shirts and capri pants in floral prints, with some taking it way over the edge by sporting sparkly visors. In the summer, they will return to their northern homes.

BEAST

(SLANG) SOMEONE WHO IS REALLY, REALLY GOOD AT SOMETHING.

SOURCES

BOOKS

Aronson, Marc and HP Newquist. *For Boys Only*. New York: Feiwel and Friends, 2007.

Glenday, Craig, ed. *Guinness World Records 2012*. New York: Random House, 2012.

Green, Aliza. *Field Guide to Seafood*. Philadelphia: Quirk Books, 2007.

Hamilton, Edith. *Mythology*. New York: Little, Brown & Co., 1942.

Hopkins, Jerry, et al. *Extreme Cuisine*. Boston: Periplus, 2004.

Kiple, Kenneth F. and Kriemhild C. Ornelas, eds. *The Cambridge World History of Food*. New York: Cambridge University Press, 2000.

Lin, Eddie. *Lonely Planet Extreme Cuisine*. London: Lonely Planet Books, 2009.

Luchetti, Emily. *A Passion for Ice Cream*. San Francisco: Chronicle Books, 2006.

Masoff, Joy. *Oh, Yuck! The Encyclopedia of Everything Nasty*. New York: Workman, 2000.

Ramos-Elorduy, Julieta. *Creepy Crawly Cuisine*. Rochester, VT: Park Street Press, 1998.

Rosenberg, Pam. *Eek! Icky, Sticky, Gross Stuff in Your Food*. North Mankato, MN: The Child's World, Inc., 2007.

Schwabe, Calvin W. *Unmentionable Cuisine*. Charlottesville, VA: University Press of Virginia, 1979.

Solheim, James. *It's Disgusting and We Ate It!* New York: Aladdin/Simon & Schuster, 1998.

Solomon, Charmaine. *Charmaine Solomon's Encyclopedia of Asian Food*. Boston: Periplus, 1998.

Tannahill, Reay. *Food in History*. New York: Three Rivers Press, 1988.

Toussaint-Samat, Maguelonne. *A History of Food*. Chichester, UK: John Wiley & Sons, 2009.

Weil, Christa. *Fierce Food*. New York: Penguin, 2006.

WEB

www.webmd.com
www.mayoclinic.com
www.nationalgeographic.com
www.animalplanet.com
www.discoverwildlife.com
www.gatorade.com
www.kidshealth.org
www.grossology.org
www.phrases.org
www.howstuffworks.com
www.mlb.com
http://en.beijing2008.cn
www.nobelprize.org
http://myfwc.com/wildlifehabitats/
    managed/alligator/
www.Einstein.biz
NPR: "The Long, Strange Journey of Einstein's
    Brain": www.npr.org/templates/story/
    story.php?storyId=4602913
www.leonardoda-vinci.org

www.hawking.org.uk
www.angesscott.edu
www.usna.edu
www.thelogics.org
www.ringling.com
www.outofafrica.nl
www.danricedays.com
www.simpsons.wikia.com
www.masaikenya.org
www.chicagotribune.com
www.imdb.com
www.cajuncrawfishpie.com
www.ASPCA.com
www.divinecaroline.com
www.gilroygarlicfestival.com
www.about.com
www.discovery.com
www.yumsugar.com
www.onekind.org
www.hotdog.org

www.ifoce.com
www.miketheheadlesschicken.org
www.johnlivereatingjohnston.com
www.wisegeek.com
www.beefheart.com
www.desertusa.com
www.applescrapple.com
www.hofbraeuhaus.de
www.spam.com
www.youtube.com: "How to Harvest Squid Ink"
www.popularscience.com
www.sheepusa.org
www.hostesscakes.com/twinkies
www.bbc.com
www.twinkiesproject.com

INFORMATION SOURCES

Montse Torremorell, University of Minnesota—information on pig intestines

MarLyn Heim, Melster Candy—Circus Peanuts

Joni Lashaway, Spangler Candy—Circus Peanuts

Michael Bohdan, Cockroach Hall of Fame—giant hissing cockroaches

Susana Trilling, Seasons of My Heart Cooking School—grasshoppers

Mario Batali—headcheese

Donald Link—headcheese

Faye Passow, Keep the Faye.com—hot-dish

Faith Farrell—hot-dish

Sabine Elisabeth Barthelmeß, Hofbräuhaus—sour lung soup and recipe

Roger Bennatti—Twinkie experiment

Robert Smith?—zombies

Emeril Lagasse—King Cake recipe

OTHER

Episodes of *Bizarre Foods*

Personal experience by Andrew Zimmern, Molly Mogren, and/or Beth Gibbs.

PHOTO CREDITS

COVER: front cover: photo of Andrew Zimmern by Gary Spector; alligator, bird's nest, dung beetle, durian, dancing shrimp, fish, garlic, hamburger, hot dog, ice cream, octopus, and Twinkie: www.istock.com; brain, crawfish, grasshopper, tarantula, tentacle, tongue, and rat: www.veer.com/images; front flap (top left): www.shutterstock.com; (top middle): courtesy of the Travel Channel; (top right): www.istock.com; (bottom left): courtesy of the Travel Channel; (bottom middle): www.shutterstock.com; (bottom right): courtesy of the Travel Channel; back cover: grasshopper, guinea pig, and tentacle: www.veer.com/images; photo of Andrew Zimmern courtesy of the Travel Channel

INTERIOR: p. 2 (top): courtesy of the Travel Channel; (bottom): www.shutterstock.com; p. 4 (left): Bocman1973/shutterstock.com; (right): NYPL/Getty Images; p. 5: www.shutterstock.com; p. 7: Gary Spector; p. 8 (top): Louise Heusinkveld/Getty Images; (bottom left): courtesy of the Travel Channel; (bottom right): www.shutterstock.com; p. 10: © Hupeng/Dreamstime.com; p. 11: www.shutterstock.com; p. 13 (top): courtesy of the Travel Channel; (bottom): www.shutterstock.com; p. 15 (top): Hulton Archive/Handout/Getty Images; (bottom): www.shutterstock.com; p 16: Associated Press; p. 17: www.shutterstock.com; p. 18: David Fowler/shutterstock.com; p. 19: www.shutterstock.com; p. 23 (Black Eyed Peas): s_bukley/shutterstock.com; (others): www.shutterstock.com; p. 24 (diagram): www.shutterstock.com; p. 26: photo by Gary Spector; p. 28: Bettmann/Corbis/AP Images; p. 29 (top): Mark Elias/Associated Press; (bottom): www.shutterstock.com; p. 31 (top): courtesy of the Travel Channel; (middle): www.shutterstock.com; p. 33: Matt Slocum/Associated Press; p. 34: courtesy of Michael Bohdan; p. 36: courtesy of the Travel Channel; p. 39: www.shutterstock.com; p. 41 (top): courtesy of the Travel Channel; p. 41: www.shutterstock.com; p. 42: www.shutterstock.com; p. 43: www.shutterstock.com; pp. 44-45: Recipe by Emeril Lagasse, courtesy Martha Stewart Living Omnimedia, Inc. For more, visit www.emerils.com; photo by Kathy Willens /Associated Press; p. 47: courtesy of the Travel Channel; p. 48: www.shutterstock.com; p. 50: www.shutterstock.com; p. 53 (Miley and Billy Ray Cyrus): Joe Seer/shutterstock.com; (others): www.shutterstock.com; p. 55 (top): courtesy of the Travel Channel; (bottom): www.shutterstock.com; p. 56: www.shutterstock.com; p. 59 (top): courtesy of the Travel Channel; (bottom): www.shutterstock.com; p. 61: www.shutterstock.com; p. 63 (top): courtesy of the Travel Channel; (bottom) www.shutterstock.com; p. 64: © Fumio Okada/Age Fotostock; p. 65 (top): Jody Kurash/Associated Press; (bottom): Kiichiro Sato/Associated Press; p. 66: Veer Images; p. 68: courtesy of the Travel Channel; p. 69: courtesy of the Travel Channel; p. 70: www.

shutterstock.com; p. 72 (top): www.shutterstock.com; p. 74: www.shutterstock.com; p. 75 (middle): John Hayes/Associated Press; (bottom): © Jim West/Age Fotostock; p. 77: courtesy of Molly Mogren; p. 78: www.shutterstock.com; p. 79: www.shutterstock.com; p. 80 (top): www.shutterstock.com; (bottom): courtesy of the Travel Channel; p. 81: www.shutterstock.com; p. 83: courtesy of the Travel Channel; p. 84: www.shutterstock.com; p. 87 (Mays): Bettmann/Corbis/AP Images; (Pujols): Kevin Hill Illustration/shutterstock.com; p. 89: www.shutterstock.com; p. 90: www.shutterstock.com; p. 91: www.shutterstock.com; p. 92: Marcela Taboada; p. 94: www.shutterstock.com; p. 95 (left): courtesy of Andrew and Molly; (right): www.shutterstock.com; p. 96 (top): s_bukley/shutterstock.com; (bottom): www.shutterstock.com; p. 99 (top left): courtesy of the Travel Channel; (top right and bottom): www.shutterstock.com; p. 100: stamp images (left): Neftali/shutterstock.com; (bottom right): Solodov Alexey/shutterstock.com; p. 101: www.shutterstock.com; p. 102: Zak Brian/SIPA/Associated Press; p. 104 (top): courtesy of the Travel Channel; (bottom): www.shutterstock.com; p. 105: www.shutterstock.com; p. 106 (top): www.shutterstock.com; (bottom): Christine V. Johnson/Associated Press; p. 107 (top): Tony Avelar/Associated Press; (bottom): www.shutterstock.com; p. 108: Alan Welner/Associated Press; p. 109 (right): spirit of america/shutterstock.com; (bottom left): www.shutterstock.com; p. 111: Matt's Bar: courtesy of Matt's Bar; the 5-8 Club: courtesy of the 5-8 Club; p. 112 (top right): © Mo-Spector/Kipa/Corbis; (top left): ABC/Getty Images; (bottom right): Bettmann/Corbis/AP Images; (bottom left): Associated Press; p. 114: www.shutterstock.com; p. 116 (top): courtesy of the Travel Channel; (bottom) www.shutterstock.com; p. 118: www.shutterstock.com; p. 119: www.shutterstock.com; p. 120: www.shutterstock.com; p. 121: www.shutterstock.com; p. 123: courtesy of the Travel Channel; p. 124: www.shutterstock.com; p. 125 (giant gummy bear): Frank Hormann/Associated Press; (all other photos): Gary Spector; p. 127: courtesy of the Travel Channel; p. 128: www.shutterstock.com; p. 129: www.shutterstock.com; p. 130: www.shutterstock.com; p. 132: courtesy of the Travel Channel; p. 133: www.shutterstock.com; p. 134 (right): s_bukley/shutterstock.com; (left): Ehab Othman/shutterstock.com; p. 136: www.shutterstock.com; p. 137: Tom Copi/Getty Images; p. 139: www.shutterstock.com; p. 140: www.shutterstock.com; p. 141: www.shutterstock.com; p. 143 (all): www.shutterstock.com; p. 145: courtesy of the Travel Channel; p. 146: © Eric Brown/Age Fotostock; p. 147: Associated Press; p. 148: www.shutterstock.com; pp. 150-151 (letters): www.shutterstock.com; p. 152: www.shutterstock.com; p. 154 (diagram and photo): www.shutterstock.com; p. 155 (top): courtesy of Hofbräuhaus München; (bottom): courtesy of the Travel Channel; p. 156: www.shutterstock.com; p. 158: www.shutterstock.com; p. 159: courtesy of the SPAM Museum; p. 160: courtesy of the Travel Channel; p. 161: courtesy of the Travel Channel; p. 163 (all): www.shutterstock.com; p. 164: www.shutterstock.com; p. 166: © Sandy Huffaker/Corbis; p. 167 (all): courtesy of the Travel Channel; p. 169: photos and diagram: www.shutterstock.com; p. 170: www.shutterstock.com; p. 171: www.shutterstock.com; p. 173 (top): www.shutterstock.com; (bottom): courtesy of the Travel Channel; p. 174: www.shutterstock.com; p. 175 (top): courtesy of the Travel Channel; (others): www.shutterstock.com; p. 177: www.shutterstock.com; p. 178 (all): www.shutterstock.com; p. 181 (top right): courtesy of the Travel Channel; (bottom) photos from *Bacon Today* by Corey James; p. 184: photo by Gary Spector; p. 185: photo by Gary Spector; p. 186: photos by Gary Spector; p. 187 (top left): www.shutterstock.com; other photos by Anna Roberto; p. 189 (top): courtesy of the Travel Channel; (bottom): www.shutterstock.com; p. 190: www.shutterstock.com; p. 192: www.shutterstock.com; p. 195: photo by Gary Spector, and hands by Anna Roberto

ACKNOWLEDGMENTS

I'm insanely proud of this book, one which couldn't have been possible without the help of many creative, funny, and smart people. Special thanks to Dusti Kugler, John Larson, Tom Wiese, the Brooks Group, and my team at WME. You all played crucial parts in turning a wild idea into reality. Beth Gibbs deserves a special mention for her tenacious dedication to this book project. After the crazy research project that became *Andrew Zimmern's Field Guide*, trust me when I say "You want her on your trivia team!" She's a rock star. To everyone who contributed photos and recipes, stories and fun facts, your personal touches brought much-appreciated depth and texture. Thank you for your generosity. I fell in love with Chuck Gonzales's illustrations the first time I saw them: funny, smart, and sometimes even a bit gross (in a good way)! Thank you for helping the text come to life. Of course, a big thanks to Jean Feiwel, Liz Szabla, and the folks at Feiwel and Friends for giving my team the opportunity to let our creativity fly, even when it was a little on the weird side, and for putting up with all my crap. You are the best. And speaking of the best, Molly Mogren . . . I adore you.

—Andrew Zimmern

INDEX